FRANZ SCHUBERT'S
LETTERS
AND OTHER WRITINGS

FRANZ SCHUBERT'S LETTERS

AND OTHER WRITINGS

*

EDITED BY
OTTO ERICH DEUTSCH

AND TRANSLATED BY
VENETIA SAVILE

WITH A FOREWORD BY
ERNEST NEWMAN

VIENNA HOUSE
New York

This Vienna House edition,
first published in 1974,
is an unabridged republication of
the work originally published by
Faber & Gwyer, London, in 1928.

International Standard Book Number: 0-8443-0028-4
Library of Congress Catalog Card Number: 73-93093

Printed in the United States of America

FOREWORD

I

Some day, perhaps, when musical criticism has been given a sounder basis in science than it has at present, the prose of composers will be utilized to throw a light on their music and *vice versa* ; but in a period when not even the basic elements of a composer's individual accent have been analysed it is rather premature to expect a scientific analysis of his prose style, still less a correlation of the prose style with the musical. But already a few of the broader resemblances between the two can be discerned in the case of a few composers. The flamboyant exaggerations of the earlier Berlioz are reproduced in his prose, with its over-exuberance of epithet and of simile—" terrible ", " frightful ", " monstrous ", " colossal ", " horrible ", Beethoven's genius soaring " like the colossal bird above the snowy summit of Chimborazo ", a success being " pyramidal ", portions of his own *Te Deum* being " Babylonian, Ninevitish ", the scene of the benediction of the poniards in *Les Huguenots* being " written as it were in electric fluid by a gigantic Voltaic pile ", and so on. The uncouth insufficiency of some of

[v]

Beethoven's first sketches for a musical work has its counterpart in the general shapelessness of his literary style. Wagner's highly involved prose, with its maddeningly long sentences, its syntactical involutions, its enclosure of one parenthetic clause in another, and then another in yet another, but with the remote end, for all that, seen clearly from the beginning, is manifestly the product of the same mind that endlessly interweaves musical motive with motive without ever losing sight for a moment of the totality of the design, however vast the span of this may be. M. Henri Bidou, though he has not worked the point out as fully as he might have done, has indicated certain fundamental resemblances of line and structure between Chopin's melodies and forms and the build of the sentences in his letters. A man's mind being all of a piece, it would indeed be surprising if the basic lines of its structure did not unconsciously reveal themselves in each one of his intellectual activities ; and some day, as I have ventured to hint, a musician's prose writings and letters will be studied not only for what he says in them but for his way of saying it, and the light this throws on the woof and warp of his musical thought.

Schubert's letters are the true counterpart of his music : the style is simple—melodic and diatonic, we may almost call it, without any involutions or complexities either of structure or of thought, expressing in the directest possible way only the broad fundamentals of things (though often, in spite of the artlessness of the prose, with something of the beauty of touch that makes his musical expression of the fundamental simplicities of feeling so magical), without anything whatever of self-consciousness or the desire to produce an effect. From his letters, as from his music, we get the impression of a nature of the utmost sweetness and simplicity,—the latter, of course, not being synonymous with superficiality ; the simplicities of a Schubert or a Mozart may go deeper than the sophistications of many a more intellectual composer. Through his letters, again, especially in the earlier period of his pitifully short life, runs that simple apposition of joy and sadness that is so characteristic of his music ; and in the letters there is generally that momentary welling over of joy into sadness and of sadness into joy that gives his music its typically Schubertian wistfulness. Some musicians seem at first sight, in their lives and their speech, to be so unlike their music that criticism is puzzled to know how to bring the man and his music into the same focus,—though criticism cannot give up the problem (that, for example, of squaring Wagner the man with Wagner the artist) without confessing the present imperfection of its instruments and its technique. But if ever there was a composer who, in his speech, showed himself to be completely like his music, it was Schubert.

Even in the sometimes tragic music of his last years there is no bitterness, only a darkening of that wistfulness that makes so much of his music so poignant. This heart-piercing wistfulness is generally concentrated, in the earlier works, in a single harmony that is a blend of sweetness and pain ; typical and familiar examples are the following passage in the andante of the Unfinished Symphony :—

and the cry of the Wanderer in the song :—

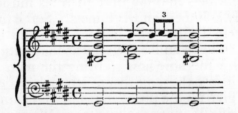

This blending of sweetness and sadness is clearly visible in his letters, though of course the nature of language does not permit of the fusion of them into a single poignant chord, as in music. But the regular concurrence of

the two mood-motives is unmistakable : if
he speaks of his joy, he sees it as a bright spot
upon the surrounding sadness of his life ; if
he is speaking of the general mournfulness of
living, his mind spontaneously reverts to the
consolations of remembered loveliness ; in
presence of the cloud he is reminded of the
silver lining, in presence of the silver lining he
is conscious of the cloud. Note the frequent
treading of the one motive on the heels of the
other in the letters :

(After hearing something of Mozart's.) " So
do these lovely impressions, which neither time
nor circumstance can efface, remain in the
mind and influence for good our whole
existence. In the dark places of life they point
to that clear-shining and distant future in which
our whole hope lies."

" Happy moments relieve the sadness of life.
Up in heaven these radiant moments will turn
into joy perpetual, and even more blessed will
be the vision of worlds more blest."

(After writing the song *Die Einsamkeit*.[1]) " I
think it is the best thing I have done, for I was
care-free when writing it."

(Lamenting the severance from Anselm
Hüttenbrenner.) " The last hope of your

---

[1] A song that is anything but " care-free " in its
entirety. The *Einsamkeit* in question is the one to words
by Mayrhofer, not the one in the *Winterreise*.

return has now flickered out. . . . I had, indeed, a presentiment when I kissed you good-bye that you would not be arriving back so soon. . . . What has become of all those supremely happy hours that we once spent together ? . . . You will have heard that otherwise everything is going very well with me."

(From his " Dream ".) " I turned on my heel, and, with a heart filled with infinite love for those who scorned it, I wandered off into a far country. For years I was torn between the greatest love and the greatest sorrow. . . . Through long, long years I sang my songs. But when I wished to sing of love it turned to sorrow, and when I wanted to sing of sorrow it was transformed for me into love. . . . I went forward, however, [to the tomb of the maiden who had died] slowly and devoutly, with my eyes lowered towards the gravestone, and before I knew it I was in the circle, from which the loveliest melody sounded. And I felt, pressed as it were into a moment's space, the whole measure of eternal bliss."

II

It seems absurd to distinguish between the youth and the mature age of a man who has died at thirty-one ; but the distinction for all that is clear enough in Schubert's case. The dividing line comes about 1823, when he was

[x]

no more than twenty-six. Till then the elasticity of youth, the keenness of youth's senses, and youth's unquenchable belief in a bright future, had sustained him through all his sufferings and privations. Apparently his most ambitious hope was never for more than a modest competency, either from the sale of his music or in some small official appointment in Vienna. Plainly, like Mozart, he was not of the stuff, either in inward being or in outward show, that can impose itself on the Philistine world : it is not unlikely that Schubert's plebeian exterior and manner stood in the way of his getting an official post, and that there was something in Mozart's insignificant appearance that made no magnate anxious to have him as his Kapellmeister, however much he may have admired the bright little man's music. It is curious to find Schubert, long after the days when the German musician had almost ceased to depend on patronage and had won for himself a definite social standing, reverting to the old type of eighteenth-century household dependant. Engaged as music teacher to the children of Count Johann Esterhazy, he submits, in 1818, to much the same conditions of wounding disesteem as those Mozart had revolted against as early as 1781, and out of which Haydn's European reputation had lifted him long before his death in 1809, while Beethoven had refused to submit to them almost from the first. Schubert at Zelez is little more than a domestic servant, living with the other servants.

He seems, however, to have felt no very great resentment at this treatment ; he had no exaggerated opinion of his general importance to the universe, and probably asked for little more from life than enough to eat and drink, a decent bed, a sympathetic friend or two, an occasional sight of the country (his letters show how sensitive he was to beautiful scenery), and money enough to pay for the vast amount of paper he needed for the absorbing business of writing music. His inner life was so warm and fragrant that he could endure a great deal from the outer world that would have meant insupportable misery to most other composers. But the illness of 1823—about the nature of which there can be little doubt—transformed his outlook. In spite of an occasional return of the old light-heartedness it is clear that during the four remaining years of his life he was never quite the same man again. The tissue he weaves out of the old paired motives of joy and sadness is now dyed in gloomier colours. In August 1823 he doubts if he will ever be perfectly well again. As the year wears on he cherishes the hope that he is cured, but in 1824 he realizes the futility of the dream. His health, he now believes, is permanently injured : " picture to yourself, I say, someone whose most brilliant hopes have come to nothing, someone to whom love and friendship are at most a source of bitterness, someone whose inspiration . . . for all that is beautiful threatens to fail, and then ask yourself if that is not a wretched and unhappy being ". He is now " oppressed by perpetual and incomprehensible longing " ; but still, as in the old days of childlike idealism, he tries " to beautify the bitter facts of existence " with his imagination,—or rather, to speak more accurately, he now tries anxiously to manufacture for himself that soothing balm of art that formerly welled unbidden from him.

By the end of 1824, although there are times when he believes his health to be improving, —and, as Schwind's letters to Schober indicate, he had managed to fill his friends with the same hope—he is subject to terrible fits of depression, and between the lines we can read that he realizes himself to be a beaten man. His imagination has difficulty now in gilding the hideous realities of life. The old simple, childlike faith in music as the sure solvent of human woes has gone. He sees the world for what it is ; only the beauties of nature bring him any consolation, and even in face of these he is saddened by the spectacle of " this vermin known as man " ; gone are the days when his heart was " filled with infinite love for those who scorned it ". By the summer of 1826 he must have begun to give up hope, in spite of the fact that he tries to assure Bauernfeld that he is " bearing up and in good spirits ". In

1827 he is looking on Vienna with very different eyes from those he had turned on the delightful city in the glad old days : now he sees only the intellectual pettiness and superficiality of the beings with whom he is condemned to spend his days. Thanks in large part to the publishers, he finds it difficult to make a decent living, while his prospects of an operatic success become fainter and fainter. His friend Mayrhofer noted the sombreness of his spirit in the early part of 1827, when he was writing the *Winterreise* ; he observes, indeed, that the mere choice of these poems was an indication of the seriousness that had taken possession of Schubert : " he had been very ill for a long time," says Mayrhofer ; " he had been through some shattering experiences, life had been stripped of its rose colour, and winter had set in for him. The irony of the poet, that had its root in wretchedness, harmonized with his own mood. I was painfully affected." Spaun also has left us a description of him at this period : " For some time Schubert had been in a gloomy state, and seemed to be hard hit (*angegriffen*) To my question what was the matter with him he only answered, ' Oh, you will soon hear and understand '."

He tries to forget his sorrows in the tavern and in musical evenings at his friends' houses, but the dark clouds gather closer about him month by month. In the summer of 1827, during a walk with Bauernfeld in which the latter had spoken joyously of his own hopes and plans, Schubert burst out, " Things are going well with you ; I can see you already as Court Councillor and famous actor. But what is to become of a poor musician like me ? In my old age I shall probably be going about from door to door like Goethe's old harper, begging my bread." There was to be no old age for him, however. He died in squalid misery in the November of the following year.

But though the tissue of his spirit took on a darker tinge in these last years, at the core it remained essentially unchanged. In his later music he plumbs depths of tragic despair that had hitherto been unknown to him ; but always, as some of the latest songs, the last chamber music, and the Mass in E flat show, the fund of deep-down sweetness in him was as rich as ever. If only he could have won through his material troubles, and, with his nature ripened and deepened by the experience of the last few years, have recovered something of his old simple acceptance of the world as a thing of love and beauty, what heart-easing music we should have had from him ! Bauernfeld has told us how, only a few days before his death, Schubert spoke to him of his plans for the future, of the " absolutely new harmonies and rhythms that were running through his head ". We get hints of these in the mournful, introspective songs of the last period, but not in the simpler and sweeter ones, that speak much the same technical language as those of the earlier years. We can only surmise what loveliness and what simple profundity there would have been in his later music had he lived.

. . . .

The present translation of the letters has been made from the edition of Professor Otto Erich Deutsch, who has devoted many years of research to assembling every document that bears upon Schubert and his environment. His great work, *Franz Schubert, die Dokumente seines Lebens und Schaffens*, must be the basis of all future biographies of the composer. In this English version are embodied some text-corrections made by Professor Deutsch in his new German edition of the correspondence, and also four letters that have not been published before. They are numbers 52, 61, 62, 68.

ERNEST NEWMAN

CONTENTS

[xvii]   B

CONTENTS

CONTENTS

[xix]

CONTENTS

[xx]

FRANZ SCHUBERT'S
LETTERS
AND OTHER WRITINGS

I. TO HIS BROTHER FERDINAND (?)

24th November, 1812

Let me bring out at once what is on my mind, so that I may come to the point and not just meander coyly round it. For a long time now I have thought over my position [1] and have found it on the whole passably good, though there is still room for improvement here and there. You know from experience how sometimes one wants to eat a roll and a few apples, and all the more when after a modest dinner one can only look forward to a wretched supper $8\frac{1}{2}$ hours later. This continually persistent wish troubles me more and more, and I must, *nolens volens*, hit upon a way of getting rid of it. The few groschen that my father allows me are all spent—the devil knows how—in the first few days. What am I to do then for the rest of the time? They who put their trust in Thee shall not be confounded. Mat-

---

[1] Written when Schubert was 15 years old from the Imperial Choristers' College, which he had entered four years earlier,

[23]

thew Chap. 3, verse 4. I thought so too—
How would it be if you were to let me have
a few kreutzers each month? You would not
really feel it, while I should consider myself
so lucky, and be quite satisfied in my cloistral
retreat. As I said before, I rely on the words
of the Apostle Matthew where he says: He
that hath two coats let him give one to the
poor. In the meantime I hope that you will
lend an ear to the voice which calls incessantly
upon you of your

> loving, poor, hopeful, once again
> poor, and not to be forgotten brother
>   FRANZ

2. TO THE MOST HONOURABLE IMPERIAL AND ROYAL CIVIC GUARD HEADQUARTERS, VIENNA

Vienna,
April, 1816

The undersigned humbly begs you to consider favourably his appointment to the vacant
post of Music Director in Laibach.

He supports his petition with the following
qualifications :—

1. He is a scholar of the Imperial and Royal
Choir School, a former chorister at the Imperial and Royal Chapel, a pupil in Composi-

tion of Herr von Salieri, Chief Kapellmeister, at whose friendly recommendation he is now seeking this post.[1]

2. He has acquired such knowledge and skill in all branches of Composition, in the practice of the organ and the violin as well as in singing that, as the enclosed certificates will show, of all candidates for this post he will be found to be the best qualified.

3. In the event of a favourable answer he solemnly promises to make the best possible use of his powers so as to give complete satisfaction.

FRANZ SCHUBERT,

at the present time Assistant Teacher at his father's
School in Vienna, Himmel-
pfortgrunde No. 10

3.   FROM HIS DIARY

13th June, 1816

All my life I shall remember this fine, clear, lovely day. I still hear softly, as from a distance, the magic strains of Mozart's music.

---

[1] Salieri's word, however, was not to be relied on. He supported another pupil, and Schubert did not get the post.

With what unbelievable power, and yet again how gently, did Schlesinger's masterly playing impress it deep, deep into one's heart ! So do these lovely impressions, which neither time nor circumstance can efface, remain in the mind and influence for good our whole existence. In the dark places of this life they point to that clear-shining and distant future in which our whole hope lies. O Mozart, immortal Mozart, how many, how infinitely many inspiring suggestions of a finer, better life have you left in our souls ! This quintet is, so to speak, one of the greatest of his lesser works.—On this occasion I too had to make my appearance. I played Variations from Beethoven, and sang Goethe's " Restless Love " and Schiller's " Amalia". Unanimous applause for the first, less for the second. I too felt that my rendering of " Restless Love " was more successful than that of " Amalia", yet it cannot be denied that the essential musicality of Goethe's poetic genius was largely responsible for the applause.

I made the acquaintance too of Mme Jenny, an exceptionally brilliant pianist, though her playing seems to lack to a certain extent genuine expression.

4. FROM THE SAME

14th June, 1816

After several months I went for an evening walk again.[1] There is nothing more agreeable, surely, than to go out into the country at the end of a hot summer's day : and for this purpose the fields between Wäring and Döbling seem specially made. In the mysterious twilight, with my brother Carl for company, I felt so happy and at peace. How lovely ! I thought, and cried aloud, and stood there enchanted. The churchyard's nearness reminded us of our dear, good mother. So, talking the while of sad and intimate things, we came to that point where the road to Döbling divides. And—as though from the Heavenly Country itself—I heard coming out of a standing post-chaise the sound of a familiar voice. I looked up—and there was Herr Weinmüller who, as he climbed out, greeted us in his own hearty and honest fashion.—Our conversation turned straightaway to the subject of outward cordiality in people's voices and talk. How some try in vain to express their

---

[1] Schubert had little time for country walks, for in addition to his school work he was obliged to give music lessons to help out his slender income, and whatever time was left over he devoted to Composition.

real feelings in just such open and heartfelt language, how the efforts of others merely turn them into a general laughing-stock. This is, one sees, a natural and not a hardly-acquired gift.

5. FROM THE SAME

15*th June*, 1816

Very often one expects too much from coming events. This was the case with me when I went to see the exhibition of national pictures held at St. Anna's.[1] Of all the pictures a Madonna and Child by Abel appealed to me most. I was much disappointed in a prince's velvet cloak. I see, moreover, that one must go more often and give more time to such things in order to get hold of the right impressions and expressions about them.

6. FROM THE SAME

16*th June*, 1816

It must be fine and inspiring for a musician to have all his pupils gathered about him, to see how each strives to give of his best in honour

---

[1] The Teachers' College of which his brother Ferdinand became later Director.

of the master's jubilee, to hear in all their compositions the simple expression of Nature, free from all that eccentricity which tends to govern most composers nowadays, and for which we are indebted—almost wholly—to one of our greatest German musicians.[1]   That eccentricity which confuses and confounds without any distinction tragic and comic, sacred and profane, pleasant and unpleasant, heroic strains and mere noise : which engenders in people not love but madness : which rouses them to scornful laughter instead of lifting up their thoughts to God.   To have banned these extravagances from the circle of his pupils, and to have kept them instead at the pure source of Nature, must be the greatest satisfaction to a musician who, following in Gluck's steps, seeks his inspiration in Nature alone, in spite of the unnatural influences of the present time.—

After fifty years spent in Vienna and nearly

[1] I.e. Beethoven.   Schubert merely voiced here the general opinion of the time.   He was influenced too by old Salieri, who saw in both Mozart and Beethoven two dangerous pioneers, and whose own warning to the musical world was : " Back to Gluck ! "   Later Schubert was to become one of Beethoven's most profound admirers.

as long in the Emperor's service, Herr Salieri celebrated his jubilee, received in recognition from His Majesty a gold medal, and held a big gathering of his scholars of both sexes. The works written for the occasion by his pupils in Composition were given in the order in which they had studied with him, from the most advanced downwards. The performance included a choral song and the oratorio " Jesu al Limbo", both by Salieri ; the oratorio modelled closely on Gluck. The occasion was interesting to all concerned.

7.   FROM THE SAME

17th June, 1816

I composed to-day for the first time for money. Namely, a cantata for Professor Wattrot von Dräxler's name-day. The fee is 100 Viennese florins.[1]

---

[1] Roughly £8 7s.   There were two currencies at this time in Austria :   (*a*) " Wiener Währung " or " Viennese currency", a system of paper money in use within the Austrian territories from the time of the national bankruptcy in 1811 until 1854 ; and (*b*) " Conventionsmünze " or " Conventional coin "—so called because based on a Convention concluded in 1753 between a number of German States, for use in international transactions.

8.   FROM THE SAME

8th September, 1816

Man is like a ball, the plaything of Chance and Passion.

This sentence seems to me to be extraordinarily true.

I have often heard it quoted : The world is like a stage where each man has his part to play. Praise and blame are awarded in the next world.—But just as theatre rôles are laid aside, so are our life rôles too, and which of us can say if he has played his well or badly ?— A bad theatre régisseur gives out parts to his people which they are not capable of playing. But there is no question of negligence with us. An actor has never been dismissed from the world-theatre, surely, because he spoke his lines badly ? As soon as he gets a suitable rôle he will play it well. Whether he is applauded or not depends on how the audience, singly and collectively, is disposed towards him. Up there [1] praise and blame depend solely on the World Régisseur. For blame is saved up too.

A man's natural disposition and education

---

[1] I.e. in heaven.

determine his intelligence and his heart. The head should be, but the heart is, the ruler. Take people as they are, not as they ought to be.

Happy moments relieve the sadness of life. Up in heaven these radiant moments will turn into joy perpetual, and ever more blessed will be the vision of worlds more blest, etc.

Happy is he who finds a trusty friend. Happier still he who finds a true friend in his wife.

Nowadays the idea of marriage is full of terrors to a single man.[1] He sees in it only dreariness or wanton sensuality. Monarchs of to-day, you see this and are silent ! Or do you fail to see it ? Then, O God ! veil in darkness our minds and our senses : yet one day draw

---

[1] A moment's pessimism, no doubt, for Schubert, aged 19, was anxious enough at that time to make Thérèse Grob his bride. His prospects, however, as Assistant Teacher were hopeless, and his failure to obtain the better-paid post at Laibach was a fresh set-back. Thérèse was plain and pock-marked—plainer even than Mozart's Constanze—but she had a good heart, and was gifted enough to sing the soprano *soli* in Schubert's earlier church music. The long letter in which he declared his love is a treasure lost to the world—and there is no other to fill the gap. Thérèse married a master-baker : and there the romance ended.

back the veil again without us having suffered harm.

Man bears misfortune without complaining, and finds it thereby the harder to bear.—Why then did God endow us with sympathy?

Light head, light heart! Excessive light-headedness usually conceals a too heavy heart.

Town-bred politeness and human sincerity are as far removed from one another as the Antipodes.

The wise man's greatest unhappiness and the fool's great happiness are grounded in custom and convention.

The noble-minded man experiences, in misfortune as in prosperity, the full measure of both.

Now I cannot think of anything more. To-morrow I shall certainly think of something else. How is that? Is my mind duller to-day than to-morrow because I am sleepy and full-fed?—Why does the mind not go on think-

ing when the body is asleep?—It surely goes
a-wandering?—It cannot sleep too?

> What strange ideas!
> Do I hear folk say?
> They cannot be solved,
> Try as we may.
> So good night
> Till morning bright.

9. DEDICATION TO JOSEF HÜTTENBRENNER [1]
WITH MS. COPY OF "THE TROUT"

Vienna,
21st February, 1818
12 o'clock at night

Dearest friend,

I am exceedingly pleased
that you like my songs. As a proof of sincerest
friendship I am sending you yet another,

---

[1] The two brothers Anselm and Josef Hüttenbrenner
from Graz were among Schubert's most faithful friends.
Anselm had thrown up the study of law in order to
devote himself to music, and he made Schubert's
acquaintance when they were both pupils of Salieri.
When his father died in 1821 he came into the family
property in Graz and only visited Vienna once more
during Schubert's lifetime. Josef, the younger brother,
served Schubert's interests with the greatest devotion.

which I have just written at midnight at Anselm Hüttenbrenner's. I wish that we could pledge our friendship in a glass of punch ! *Vale.*

Just now when I wanted to sprinkle sand quickly over the thing, I took up instead, half drunk with sleep, the ink-stand and poured it all over. What a disaster !

10. TO ANSELM HÜTTENBRENNER

Vienna,
19*th March,* 1818

Dear Hüttenbrenner,

Please do your utmost to be at home next Thursday afternoon, the 19th of the month that is, at 3 o'clock, so that

---

For a time they lodged in the same house, and Josef carried on noble rescue work among Schubert MS. compositions which friends were in the habit of carrying off and never returning. In this way he collected over 100 songs which the composer himself had made no effort to recover. Hüttenbrenner was responsible for several pianoforte arrangements of Schubert's works, and for a time he even took over the thankless task of battling with publishers and theatre-managers, etc., on behalf of the struggling musician. A third brother, Heinrich, wrote poems in Graz, and one or two of these Schubert set to music.

I can come and call for you, and we can then go on to the Kunzes together. If you should not have time—but that would badly upset my plans—then leave word for me with your landlord. This is the urgent request of your friend,

FRANZ SCHUBERT

11. TO SCHOBER AND THE OTHER FRIENDS

Zelez,[1]
3rd August, 1818

Dearest and best Friends,

How could I possibly forget you—you who are everything to me! Spaun, Schober, Mayrhofer, Senn, how are you all? Are you all well? I am in the best of health. I live and compose like

---

[1] Schubert was never cut out for the year-in year-out drudgery of a school-teacher's life, and in the autumn of 1817 he made a bid for freedom. His father, however, with an eye to the family finances, persuaded him to ask for a year's leave instead. This Schubert obtained—but without pay. In order to eke out a livelihood he accepted the post of music master to the two daughters of Count Johann Esterhazy. The Esterhazy family spent the summer on their Hungarian estate at Zscliz, and this time Schubert went too.

[36]

a god, as though indeed nothing else in the world were possible.

Mayrhofer's " Loneliness " is finished, and I think it is the best thing I have done, for I was care-free when writing it. I hope you are all as well and happy as I am. I am really alive at last, thank God ! It was high time, for otherwise I should have merely become just another worthless musician. Let Schober pay my respects to Herr Vogl.[1] Next time I will make so bold as to write to him too. Ask him some time, if the chance occurs, if he would have the kindness to sing one of my songs—whichever he likes—at the Kunzes' concert in November. Greetings to everyone you can think of. My humblest respects to your mother and sister. Write very soon, all of you : every word from you is precious.

Your ever faithful friend,

FRANZ SCHUBERT

---

[1] When Schober brought about a meeting between Schubert and the opera singer Michael Vogl, the latter was already at the height of his fame. This meeting, upon which so much depended, fulfilled its object. Vogl recognized in the clumsy and speechless young man at the piano a new genius, and undertook to bring his songs before the public—though with certain alterations and ornamentations of his own.

[37]

12. TO HIS BROTHER FERDINAND

24th August, 1818

Dear brother Ferdinand,

It is half past eleven at night, and your " Requiem " is finished. It made me sad enough, believe me, for I put my whole soul into the writing of it. You must add the finishing touches wherever they are lacking : for instance, fill in the text under the stave, and the musical signs above it. If you want to put in some repeats, do so without consulting me about it at Zeliz. Things are not going well with you : I wish I could change with you so as to make you happy for once. You would find relief from every heavy burden. Dear brother, I wish with all my heart it were possible—— My foot has gone to sleep, and that is very annoying. If the silly thing could write, it wouldn't fall asleep. . . . Good morning, little brother ! I fell asleep as well as my foot and am now continuing this letter on the 25th at 8 o'clock in the morning. I have a request to make in exchange for yours : Give greetings to my dear parents, brothers and sisters, friends and acquaintances, in particular not forgetting Karl. Did he not mention me in his letter ? . . . Stir up

[38]

my friends in town to write to me, or get someone else to give them a really sharp reminder. Tell Mother [1] that my linen is well looked after, and that I am very sensible of her maternal care. (Though, if a further supply were possible, I should be very pleased if you could send me some handkerchiefs, neck-scarves and stockings. I badly need two pairs of cashmere trousers as well. Hart could take the measurements from anything of mine he likes. I would send the money for them at once.) I received during July, inclusive of travelling expenses, 200 florins.

It is already beginning to be cold here, nevertheless we shall not set out for Vienna before the middle of November. Next month I hope to go on a few weeks' visit to Freystadtl, the property of Count Erdödy, uncle to my Count. [2] The country about there is said to be exceptionally pretty. I hope to get to Pest too, for we shall be at Bosczmedjer for the vintage, and it is not far from there. I should be extremely glad if a meeting with the Ad-

[1] This was his father's second wife, who was always very good to Schubert. His own mother died when he was 15.

[2] I.e. Count Johann Esterhazy.

ministrator Herr Taigele were possible then. Above all I am looking forward to the vintage feasts, for I have heard so many merry stories about them. The harvest here is very interesting too. The corn is not gathered, as in Austria, into barns, but is stacked in the open fields in what they call "Tristen". These stacks are often 40 to 50 *klafters*[1] long, and 15 to 20 high. They are built so skilfully that the rain runs off them without doing any damage. Oats and such-like are buried underground too.—In spite of everything going well, and my health being good, and the people here being so kind, I am counting the days till the word goes forth: To Vienna! To Vienna! Yes, beloved Vienna, you hold in your narrow compass the dearest and most precious things in my life, and nothing but the blessed sight of them again will put an end to my longing. Once again please do not forget my wish mentioned above.

Heartiest greetings to my aunt Schubert and daughter.	I remain with love to all your true and faithful FRANZ. A thousand greetings to your good wife and dear little Resi.

---

[1] A *klafter* measures about 2½ yards.

13.   TO SCHOBER AND THE OTHER FRIENDS

8th September, 1818

Dear Schober,[1]   Dear Senn,
Dear Spaun,   Dear Streinsberg,
Dear Mayrhofer,   Dear Wayss.
        Dear Weidlich,

How infinitely happy your letters, separately and together, make me is beyond telling. I was attending a cattle auction when they brought me in your fat budget. I opened it and, catching sight of Schober's name, gave vent to a loud cry of joy. With childish pleasure and laughing to myself all the time, I read it through in a room near-by. It was as though my dearest friends were really within arm's reach again ! But now I must answer you all in the proper order.

---

[1] Schubert first met the budding poet, Franz von Schober, through their mutual friend Spaun. Schober was at that time a clever and artistic worldling, but in spite of the differences in their characters and circumstances, he became one of Schubert's closest friends. His own talents found a natural development in the Schubertian circle. Later he became an actor, and left Vienna for a somewhat adventurous life in Breslau. Schubert set over a dozen of his poems to music.

Dear Schobert,

I see that this alteration in your name holds good. Well, dear Schobert, your letter was from beginning to end very precious and delightful, and especially the last sheet. Yes, indeed, the last sheet sent me into the Seventh Heaven of joy. You are a splendid fellow (in Swedish of course), and, believe me, my friend, you will not fail, for your understanding of art is the finest and sincerest imaginable. That you should look upon this change as a small one pleases me very much : for a long time now you have had one foot in our particular inferno.—The fact that the management of the Opera-house in Vienna is so stupid and produces the finest operas but none of mine, makes me pretty furious. Here in Zelez I have to be everything at once. Composer, editor, audience, and goodness knows what besides. There is not a soul here with a genuine interest in music except, perhaps, now and then, the Countess (if I am not mistaken). So I am all alone with my beloved, and must hide her in my room, in my pianoforte, and in my own heart. Although this is often very depressing, yet on the other hand it inspires me towards greater things. Do not be afraid that I shall stay away any longer than I absolutely must. Several new songs—and I hope very successful ones—have come into being during this time. That the bird of Greece [1] should be fluttering his wings in Upper Austria does not surprise me at all, since it is his own country and he is on a holiday. I wish I were with him. I should certainly know how to make good use of my time. But that you—by nature a sensible fellow—should imagine my brother to be wandering about there alone, with neither guide nor companion, does surprise me very much. First, since an artist likes best of all to be left to himself; 2nd, since there are too many lovely districts in Upper Austria for him not to be able to discover the most beautiful; 3rd, since he has an agreeable acquaintance in Herr Forstmeyer in Linz. He must know quite certainly, therefore, what he is about. [2]

If you could manage a greeting to Max, when his melancholia is better, I should be infinitely glad. And since you will shortly be seeing your mother and sister, please give them my kindest regards. It is quite possible

---

[1] An allusion to Vogl's love of the classics.
[2] Schubert's reasoning is not very clear !

that this letter will not reach you in Vienna in time, for I only received yours at the beginning of September, just when you were due to leave.[1] I will then have it sent on to you. I am very glad, among other things, that Milder [2] is, for you, irreplaceable. I feel the same about her too. She sings best and trills worst of all.

Now a description for you all :

Our castle is by no means one of the largest, but it is very attractively built. It is surrounded by a lovely garden. I live in the estate agent's house. It is fairly quiet except for some forty geese, which at times set up such a cackling that one cannot hear oneself speak. All the people about me are thoroughly kind-hearted. It is rare for a nobleman's household to run as smoothly as this one. The agent, a Slav from Slavonia and a good fellow,

[1] Schober's home was the castle Torup near Malmö and he went back to Sweden for a year.

[2] Anna Milder-Hauptmann was " discovered " by Schikaneder, studied under Salieri, and became in her time one of the stars of the Viennese Opera. She was both a great singer and an excellent actress, and it was for her that Beethoven wrote the rôle of Fidelio. Schubert first heard her sing when he was at the Choir College, and the deep impression she made on him then never faded.

very much fancies his former musical talents.
He can blow on the lute two German dances
in a masterly fashion. His son, a student of
philosophy, has just arrived on his holidays, and
I hope I shall get on very well with him.
His wife is just like any other woman who
wants to be taken for a lady. The steward is
perfectly suited to his job : a man of extraordinary perspicacity in whatever concerns his
own purse and pocket. The doctor, twenty-
four years old, and a really able man, is as full
of ailments as an old lady. A great deal of it
put on. The surgeon, whom I like best of all,
a venerable old man of seventy-five, always
happy and serene. God grant to all such a
fortunate old age ! The magistrate a very
unaffected and pleasant man.[1] A cheerful old
bachelor, companion to the Count, and a
good musician, often comes to see me. The
chef, the lady's maid, the chambermaid, the
lodge-keeper, etc., and two coachmen are all
good folk. The chef, rather a loose fellow ;
the lady's maid, 30 years old ; the chambermaid very pretty, and often in my company ;
the children's nurse a nice old body ; the

[1] The great Hungarian landowners at that time had
legal powers of jurisdiction on their own estates.

lodge-keeper my rival. The two grooms are better suited to the stables than to human society. The Count is rather a rough sort of man, the Countess proud, but a more sensitive nature, the little Countesses good children. So far I have been spared any invitation to the dining-room.[1] I can think of nothing more to tell you now. I need hardly say to all of you that know me that with my naturally frank disposition I get along very well with all these people.

Dear Spaun, I am heartily glad that you are able at last to build palaces for little clerks of the Court Chancery to run about in. You probably mean by this a choral quartet. Remember me to Herr Gahy.

Dear Mayerhofer, you cannot be longing for November much more than I am. Stop being so seedy, or at least give up taking medicine, and the other will follow of itself.

For Hans Senn to read too if he pleases : as above.

Maybe friend Streinsberg is already dead :

---

[1] So Mozart, when he was in the service of the Cardinal Archbishop of Salzburg, had his place in the servants' hall " above the archbishop's cooks but below the archbishop's valets ". (*Mozart's Operas*, by E. J. Dent, p. 109. Chatto and Windus, 1913.)

and that is why he cannot write. Let friend
Weidlich tack his name on to his own coat-tails.

Good old Waiss remembers me with gratitude. He is an excellent man.

And now, dear friends, good-bye. Write
to me very soon. My best and favourite form
of entertainment is to read your letters through
a dozen times.

Greetings to my dear parents, and tell them
how much I long for a letter from them.
With enduring love,

Your faithful friend,

FRANZ SCHUBERT

Via   c/o Count
Raab   Johann Esterhazy,
and   in
Torok.   Zelez,

14.   TO HIS BROTHERS AND SISTER, FERDINAND,
IGNAZ, AND THÉRÈSE

Zelez,
29*th October*, 1818

Dear brother Ferdinand,

The sin of appro-
priation was already forgiven you in my first
letter. You had no reason, therefore, unless
it was your tender conscience, for putting off

[47]

writing so long. My Requiem pleased you, you wept during the performance of it, and perhaps at just the same passage as I. My dear brother, that is the highest reward possible for this gift of mine : do not let me hear you speak of any other.—If I did not get to know the people about me here better each day, I might be just as contented as I was at the beginning. But I see now that with the exception of one or two really good-hearted girls I have nothing in common with any of them. I long for Vienna more and more each day. We shall set out in the middle of November. Loving greetings and kisses to those dear little creatures Pepi and Marie, and also to my parents. My friends in town are very neglectful. So long as Schober's wish dies out a secret, I do not mind.

The musical events leave me fairly cold. I am only amazed at the blind and topsy-turvy zeal of my somewhat clumsy friend Doppler. He hinders rather than helps me with his friendship. As for me, I shall never turn my inmost feelings to personal or political account : what I feel in my heart I give to the world, and there is an end of it.

By all means have my pianoforte moved over to you. I shall be very glad. I am only vexed that you should fancy I do not like your letters. It is dreadful to think such a thing of your brother, and still more to write it. But what does displease me is that you are always speaking of payments and rewards and thanks, and that between brothers . . . oh, hateful !—Kisses to your dear wife and your little Resi. Fare you well !

Ignaz and Resi, I am so happy at getting letters from you both. You, Ignaz, are still the same old man of iron. Your implacable hatred of all the tribe of bonzes [1] does you credit. You have no notion, though, what the parsons round here are like : bigoted as cattle, stupid as jack-asses, mannerless as buffaloes. You hear sermons, in comparison with which the so highly venerated Father Nepomucene is nothing. They fling out from the pulpit such epithets as : " Worthless baggages ! Rabble ! " etc., until it is really a pleasure to listen. Or they bring up a skull into the pulpit with them, and say : " Look at this, you sun-blotched mugs ! That is what you will be like one of these days." Or : " See that lad ! There he goes with his wench into the tavern. They dance the whole night through, and then fall

---

[1] In this instance the clergy.

D

tipsy into bed together : and soon there'll be three of them," etc., etc.—I wonder if you thought of me during the festivities.—You often think of me, dear Resi; that is charming.—I send ninety-nine kisses apiece to the Holepeins both husband and wife, to Resi and Heinrich and Carl, and to his godfather and the godfather's future wife. Whether or not I have thought of you will be answered in person

by

FRANZ HIMSELF

15. TO ANSELM HÜTTENBRENNER IN GRÄTZ

Vienna,
21*st January,* 1819

Dear old friend,

Are you still alive ? When I consider how long it is since you have been away and since you have written and how faithlessly you have abandoned us, I really feel obliged to ask.

The last hope of your return has now flickered out. What on earth keeps you bound hand and foot in that cursed Grätz ? Have you fallen under some spell that holds you captive in its terrible ban, and makes you forget all the rest of the world? I had, indeed, a presentiment when I kissed you good-bye that you would not be coming back so soon again.

You have composed two symphonies: that is good. You let us see nothing of them: that is not good. You should really let your old friend hear something of you now and again.

What has become of all those supremely happy hours that we once spent together? Perhaps you do not think of them any more. But how often do I! You will have heard that otherwise everything is going very well with me.

I wish you with all my heart the same.

Be my friend always and do not forget

Your

SCHUBERT

Write to me really soon.

16. TO THE SAME

Vienna,

19th May, 1819

Dear friend,

A rogue — that's what you are !!! Ten years will probably slip past before you see Vienna again. First one girl and then another turns his head. Oh, may the devil take the lot, if you let them bewitch you so ! For God's sake get married, and then there will be an end of it.—You certainly can say like Caesar : Rather the first in Grätz than the second in Vienna. Well, be that as it may, I am in a raging fury that you are not here. The proverb quoted above applies even more to Cornet than to you. God give him joy of it ! Finally I shall come to Grätz as well and play the rival to you.—There is little news here. If one hears anything good it is sure to be old.—Rossini's " Othello " was given here a short time ago. Except for Radichi it was all very well done. It is a far better, that is to say, a far more characteristic opera than " Tancred ". His extraordinary creative genius is undeniable. The orchestration is at times highly original, and the vocal parts too, and, except for the usual Italian *galopades* and several reminiscences of " Tancred ".—In spite of Vogl it is hard to outmanœuvre such rabble as Weigl, Treitschke, etc. So instead of my operette [1]

---

[1] " The Twin Brothers ", a musical comedy in one act. This was not a very propitious moment for Schubert, for Rossini was all the rage in Vienna. The operetta was put on one side until 1820, when it was given six times with Vogl in the chief part.

other wretched stuff is being given that makes one's hair stand on end.

Catel's " Semiramis " with wonderfully fine music is to be performed next.—Herr Stümer, a tenor from Berlin, who has already sung in several operas, will make his first appearance here. His voice is rather weak ; no low tones, and continual falsetto in the upper register— I cannot think of anything else now. Work hard at your composition, and let us too have a share in it.

Fare you well.   Your true friend,

Vienna, 19*th May*, 1819.   FRANZ SCHUBERT

17.   TO JOSEF HÜTTENBRENNER

Vienna,
1819 (?)

Dear Hüttenbrenner,

I am yours now and always. I am extremely glad that the symphony [1] is ready. Bring it round to me this evening, at 5 o'clock let us say. I am living in the Wipplingerstrasse with Mayrhofer.

---

[1] Josef Hüttenbrenner had arranged it for pianoforte.

18. TO HIS BROTHER FERDINAND

Steyr,
15*th July,* 1819

Dear Brother

I trust that this letter will find you in Vienna and in the best of health. I am really writing to ask you to send me as soon as possible the " Stabat Mater ", which we want to perform here. I am very well so far, only the weather is persistently unfavourable. Yesterday, the 12th, a very bad thunderstorm broke over Steyr, and the lightning killed a girl and paralysed two men in the arm. In the house where I am lodging there are eight girls, nearly all pretty. So you see one is kept busy ! Herr von K[oller], with whom Vogl and I have our meals every day, has a very pretty daughter, who is a good pianist and is learning to sing several of my songs.

Please have the enclosed letter sent on. You see I am not nearly so faithless as you perhaps imagine !

Greetings to my parents and brothers and sisters, to your wife and to all my acquaintances. Do not forget the " Stabat Mater ". The country about Steyr is   Your
unimaginably lovely.   ever faithful
                                              brother, FRANZ

19. TO JOHANN MAYRHOFER [1]

Linz,
19*th August,* 1819

Dear Mayrhofer,

If you are as well as I am, then you are in excellent health. At the present moment I am in Linz. I was at the Spauns', met Kenner, Kreil, and Forst-mayer, got to know Spaun's mother, and also Ottenwald, to whom I sang his " Cradle-song " with my own setting. I enjoyed myself very much in Steyr, and mean to do so again. The country there is heavenly, and round Linz it is lovely too. We—that is to say Vogl and I—are setting out for Salzburg in a few

---

[1] Schubert met Mayrhofer when he himself was 17 and the poet just 10 years older. They became friends at once, and later shared the same room in Vienna for two years. Mayrhofer supplied the text for a great number of Schubert's songs. By nature a free-lance and an artist, Mayrhofer was obliged to spend his life as a book-auditor whose task was to take care that no censored books were sold, whereas the Censor had to review and criticize them. He was not strong and had none of the *joi-de-vivre* of the other friends. A few years after Schubert's death he developed melancholia and took his own life.

days' time. I am looking forward so much to
. . . I recommend to your kindness the
bearer of this letter. He is a student from
Kremsmünster named Kahl, and is passing
through Vienna on the way to his parents in
Idria. Please let him have my bed during
the time that he is there. I hope that you
will do your best to make him welcome in
every way, for he is a very good and friendly
creature.

Heartiest greetings to Frau von S[ansouci].
Have you written anything yet? I am hoping
so.[1]—We celebrated Vogl's birthday with a
cantata for which Stadler wrote the words
and I the music, and it was a great success.
Now good-bye until the middle of September.

Herr v. Vogl wishes to be   Your
remembered to you.   friend,
Greetings to   FRANZ SCHUBERT
Spaun.

---

[1] Schubert was anxious to get to work on an opera
libretto.

20.   TO JOSEF VON SPAUN [1]

Vienna,
2nd November, 1821

Dear friend,

I was very pleased to have your letter, and I hope that everything will continue to go pleasantly for you.—I must tell you that my dedications have not missed their mark : namely, the Patriarch has been good for 12 ducats, and Friess on Vogl's intervention for 20, which is splendid for me. [2]

So you must be good enough to end your correspondence with the Patriarch with an expression of thanks suitable both to his

[1] Schubert's friendship with Spaun, who was nine years his senior, dated from the Choir College days when they played second violin together in the school orchestra at the same desk.

[2] In Ignaz von Sonnleithner, barrister and lover of the fine arts, Schubert had found an energetic champion. His son Leopold conceived the idea of having Schubert's songs printed gradually by private subscription. The second set to appear was dedicated to Count Moritz von Friess, and the fourth set to Ladislaus Pyrker von Felsö-Eör, Patriarch of Venice. The songs sold well enough to become a steady if modest source of income for Schubert. Ignaz von Sonnleithner's brother Josef was also Schubert's patron.

position and to mine.—Schober's opera is already successfully written up to the 3rd act, and I very much wish that you could be here during its composition.[1] We expect a great deal from it.—The Kärnthnertor-and Wieden Theatre is really leased to Barbaja, and he takes it over on the 2nd December. Now good-bye. Remember me to everyone, and especially to your sister and brother.

Your friend,

FRZ. SCHUBERT

Write soon to the Patriarch and to us.

N.B. Send me Ottenwald's "Cradle-song".

21. TO JOSEF HÜTTENBRENNER

Vienna,

1822

Will you be so good as to bring me out the acts of the opera one at a time for correction ?

---

[1] Schober wrote the (very weak) libretto and Schubert the music of "Alfonso and Estrella". When Weber came to Vienna he made vague promises for its production in Dresden, and on the strength of this Schubert had a second copy made by his publisher Diabelli for 100 gulden. In vain. The opera was performed for the first time thirty-two years later in Weimar, with Liszt conducting, once again sixty years later in Berlin : and that was the end of it.

I wish you would also see how my account stands with Diabelli, for I am in need of money.

SCHUBERT

22. ALLEGORICAL STORY [1]

3rd July, 1822

MY DREAM

I was one of many brothers and sisters. We had a good father and mother. I felt a deep love for them all.—One day my father took us to a feast. My brothers became very merry there. But I was sad. My father then came up to me and bade me taste the delicious foods. But I could not, and at that my father in his anger banished me from his sight. I turned on my heel, and, with a heart filled with infinite

---

[1] Founded closely on fact. When Schubert was still at the Choir College he neglected his other studies for music, and as a punishment, it is supposed, his father forbade him the house. Elisabeth Schubert's sudden death softened her husband's heart. The ban was removed, and Franz was even permitted to study under Salieri. The second quarrel between father and son, which lasted three years, broke out in 1818 when Schubert refused to return to the " pleasure-garden ", otherwise the School-house, and went off instead to Zelez.

[59]

love for those who scorned it, I wandered off
into a far country. For years I was torn
between the greatest love and the greatest
sorrow. Then came news of my mother's
death. I hastened back to see her, and my
father, softened by grief, did not hinder my
return. I saw her lying dead. Tears poured
from my eyes. I saw her lying there, looking
just as she used to, one with the dear past in
which, according to her wishes, we ought still
to live and move and have our being.

We followed her mourning to the grave, and
the coffin slowly sank.—From this time on-
wards I stayed at home again. Then one
day my father took me once more into his
pleasure-garden. He asked me if it pleased
me. But the garden was hateful to me, and I
did not dare to reply. Then he asked me a
second time, and more impatiently, if I liked
the garden.—Trembling I told him no. At
that my father struck me and I fled. For
the second time I turned away, and, my heart
filled with infinite love to those who scorned
it, I wandered once more into distant lands.
Through long, long years I sang my songs.
But when I wished to sing of love it turned to
sorrow, and when I wanted to sing of sorrow
it was transformed for me into love.

So was I divided between love and sorrow. And once a pious maiden who had just died appeared to me. And a circle formed about her tomb in which many youths and old men wandered as though in perpetual bliss. They spoke softly so as not to wake the maiden.

Heavenly thoughts like bright sparks seemed to flicker unceasingly out of the virgin's tomb, and to fall in a soft-sounding shower on to the young men. I longed to walk there too. But only by a miracle, so people said, could one enter the circle. I went forward, however, slowly and devoutly, with my eyes lowered towards the gravestone, and before I knew it I was in the circle, from which the loveliest melody sounded. And I felt, pressed as it were into a moment's space, the whole measure of eternal bliss. My father I saw too, loving and reconciled. He folded me in his arms and wept. And I still more.

FRANZ SCHUBERT

23. TO JOSEF HÜTTENBRENNER
Dear Hüttenbrenner,

As I have to make some very important alterations in the songs which I handed over to you, do not give them to Herr Leidesdorf yet, but bring them back to me here instead. Should they have been already sent to him, they must be fetched back as soon as possible.

FRZ. SCHUBERT

Vienna. 31*st October,* 1822.

24. TO JOSEF VON SPAUN

Vienna,

7*th December,* 1822

Dear Spaun,

I hope that the dedication of these three songs will give you a little pleasure. You deserve so much more for all that you have done for me [1] that I really ought to give you, *ex-officio*, something infinitely greater, and I would too if only I were in a position to do so. You will be satisfied with the selection, for I have chosen out those songs which you yourself specified. Two other sets are appearing at the same time : one is already printed, and I have put aside a copy for you, and the other is actually in the printer's hands. The first set contains, as you will see, the " Three Songs of the Harp-player ", of which the second, " Who never ate his bread with

---

[1] Spaun had brought about a reconciliation between Schubert and his father.

tears ", is new, and has been dedicated to the Bishop of St. Pölten, and the other contains, as you will *not* see, " Suleika " and " Secrets " and is dedicated to Schober. In addition to these I have also composed a fantasia for the pianoforte (for two hands) which is being printed too, and is dedicated to a certain rich person. I have also set to music some more of Goethe's poems, for instance : " The Child of the Muses ", " To the Absent One ", " By the River ", and " Welcome and Farewell ".— As to my opera, there is nothing to be looked for in Vienna. I asked for, and received, it back again : Vogl too has definitely left the theatre. I shall send it shortly either to Berlin or to Dresden, from which last Weber has sent me a most encouraging letter.— My Mass is finished and will be given before long. I still cling to the old idea of dedicating it either to the Emperor or to the Empress, for I feel it is a good piece of work.—Now I have told you all I can about myself and my music ;—let me add some news about someone else. " Libussa ", a big opera by C. Kreutzer, has just been performed here for the first time, and was a success. The second act is supposed to be especially fine. I only heard the first, which left me cold.

And now, how are you ? I certainly hope well, and so I may perhaps be forgiven this tardy enquiry. How are your family ? What is Streinsberg doing ?—Write and tell me about everything really soon. If I were not so vexed over this shameful business with the opera, I should be fairly content. Now that Vogl has left the theatre and my troubles in that direction are consequently over, I have taken up with him again. I hope either to accompany— or follow—him into the country again this summer : and am looking forward to this very much, for I shall see you and your friends again.—Our life together in Vienna is very pleasant nowadays. We meet at Schober's every week for three readings and a Schubertiade at which Bruchmann appears too. And now good-bye, dear Spaun. Write to me very soon and fully, so that the yawning void which your absence will always make about me may be at least partially filled. Remember me to your brothers, and give warmest greetings to your sister and Ottenwald as well as to Streinsberger and all the others, etc.

Your faithful friend,

FRANZ SCHUBERT

Address your letter to the School-house,

[64]

Grünthorgasse, in the Rossau, for that is where
I am living now.

25.   TO LEOPOLD VON SONNLEITHNER

Vienna,

January, 1823 (?)

Dear Herr von Sonnleithner,

You know your-
self how it was with the reception of the
latest [vocal] quartets : people have had
enough of them. It is possible that I might
succeed in discovering a new *genre*, but even
then one could not reckon with certainty on
its success.[1] Since my future career is a
matter of some importance to me, you, who
flatter me with an interest in it too, will be
bound to admit that I must make my way in
security and that it is, therefore, quite impossible for me to accept the honour of this
invitation—unless, indeed, the Society would
be contented with Jaeger's rendering of the
Romance from " The Magic Harp ", and so
restore the peace of mind of

Yours sincerely,

FRZ. SCHUBERT

---

[1] His highly original " Song of the Spirits " for men's
voices, unaccompanied, had been received by the
Viennese in silence.

26. TO JOSEF PEITL (?)

[Undated]

Dear Herr von Bäutel,[1]

Since I possess nothing for a full orchestra which I could send out with a quiet conscience into the world, and since there are so many selections from the great masters to choose from—for example, Beethoven's Overtures from " Prometheus ", " Egmont ", " Coriolanus ", etc., etc., —I must heartily beg your forgiveness for not being able to help you in this matter, for it could only be prejudicial to me to appear with something mediocre. Please forgive, therefore, my too hasty and unconsidered consent.

Yours sincerely,

FRZ. SCHUBERT

27. TO ANTON DIABELLI

Vienna,
21st February, 1823

Herr von Diabelli,

I enclose the quartet together with the pianoforte accompaniment.

[1] Schubert's spelling, even of proper names, was often more phonetic than correct.

The appearance of the two books of Waltzes has somewhat surprised me, as their publication is not in complete accordance with the agreement. A suitable remuneration would not be out of place.

Please let me have the account for the last three volumes as well, for I am thinking of closing with you in this matter, and, if you are willing, am prepared to make over all copyrights of the same to you for 300 Viennese florins.[1]

Kindly let me have too a few more copies of the Fantasia.

FRANZ SCHUBERT

28. TO IGNAZ FRANZ VON MOSEL

Honoured Herr Hofrat,

Pray forgive me for troubling you again with a letter, but the state of my health does not yet allow me to venture out of doors.

I have the honour to send you now, Herr Hofrat, the 3rd and last Act of my opera,

---

[1] Thus in a weak moment Schubert brought to nothing the whole of Leopold Sonnleithner's well-thought-out scheme.

and also the Overture to the 1st Act, with the request that you will be so good as to let me have your opinion on it. Should I still be unable to see you in person, would you please indicate when I could send for the whole opera together with your criticism of it. May I remind you, Herr Hofrat, of your most kind promise of a letter of recommendation to Weber, and may I go further and venture to ask you now, if you see your way to do so, to return my opera with a similar covering letter to Baron von Könneritz, who according to Weber is Manager of the Theatre in Dresden.

And now, Herr Hofrat, since I am troubling you with so many requests, may I very humbly add this last one, namely, that you would be so kind as to let me have in the mean-time the opera text-book destined by you for my unworthy self, for I solemnly promise to take all possible care of it and to let nobody so much as have a glimpse of it.

With the deepest respect,
I remain, Herr Hofrat,
Your most obedient servant,
FRANZ SCHUBERT

Vienna. 28th February, 1823.

[68]

29. TO CAPPI AND DIABELLI

Gentlemen,

Your letter has indeed surprised me, for I understood from Herr von Cappi's own statement that the account was completely settled. During the earlier negotiations over the publication of the Waltzes I became aware of the not over-scrupulous intentions of my publishers, and their conduct, therefore, on this second occasion is easy to explain : and you gentlemen yourselves will have no difficulty in the circumstances in finding a natural explanation for the long contract which I have now entered into with another publisher. Neither am I able to understand your suggestion of a debt of 150 Viennese florins, for the estimate you gave me for copying the opera only amounted to 100 florins. Be that as it may, I feel that the extremely small purchase price which you paid for my earlier things, including the Fantasia at 50 florins, long ago wiped out this debt which you so unjustly put upon me. However, since I very much doubt whether you will take so human and reasonable a view, I am compelled to call your attention to my legal right to 20 copies of the latest and 12 copies of the earlier sets of songs, and my even more justifiable claim to repayment of the 50 florins which you knew how to get out of me in so extremely ingenious a way. Kindly reckon all this together and you will find that my claim is not only greater than yours but fairer too, though I should never have made it, had you not reminded me of it in such an unpleasant fashion. As you will be good enough to see for yourselves, my debt was wiped out in this way long ago, nor can there be any question whatever of your publishing any more of my songs, whose worth *you* could never estimate cheaply enough, though I now receive 200 Viennese florins a volume for them. Herr von Steiner too has made me several offers of publication for my works. In conclusion I must ask you please to send me back all my manuscripts, the engraved as well as the unengraved works.

Yours faithfully,

FRZ. SCHUBERT
Composer

10*th April*, 1823.

N.B. Please let me have an exact account of the number of copies delivered to me since our first sales-agreement, for I find that my calculation greatly exceeds yours.

[70]

30.   TO SCHOBER

Steyr,
14*th August*, 1823

Dear Schober,

Although I am rather late in writing I hope, nevertheless, that this letter may still find you in Vienna.   I am in constant correspondence with Schäffer and am in fairly good health, though I rather doubt ever becoming perfectly well again.   I lead here a very simple life in every way, take plenty of exercise, work hard at my opera, and read Walter Scott.

I get on admirably with Vogl.   We were together in Linz, where he sang a great deal and very well.   Bruchmann, Sturm, and Streinsberg visited us in Steyr a few days ago, and were sent off too with a fresh load of songs.   I shall hardly see you before your journey home, so I must wish you now again and again all luck in your undertaking and assure you of my never-failing love, which will suffer unspeakably in your absence.   Let me hear something of you from time to time wherever you may be.

Your friend,

FRANZ SCHUBERT

To Kupelwieser, Schwind, Mohn, etc., etc.,

to the [unreadable] already . . . written to, kindest remembrances.

My address : Steyr, c/o H. v. Vogl.

31. TO THE STYRIAN MUSICAL SOCIETY

Honoured Musical Society,

I sincerely thank you for the Honorary Member's diploma which you have been so good as to send me, and which, on account of my long absence from Vienna, I only received a few days ago.

May my devotion to the art of music succeed in making me worthy one day of this distinction. In order to express my liveliest thanks in music as well I will make so bold as to present your honoured Society at the earliest possible date with the score of one of my Symphonies.[1]

With the deepest respect I remain,

The Society's most grateful and

devoted servant,

FRANZ SCHUBERT

Vienna. 20th September, 1823.

---

[1] A year elapsed, however, before Schubert, after a reminder from his father, sent off the Symphony in B minor to Anselm Hüttenbrenner, who was Director of the Society. For some inexplicable reason Anselm Hüttenbrenner never produced it, nor did Schubert

32. TO SCHOBER

Vienna,
30th November, 1823

Dear Schober,

I have been longing to write to you for some time now, but I never could find a moment. You yourself know how it is.

First of all I must send you my laments over the sad state of our Society [1] and indeed over all other conditions here, for, except for my health, which seems at last (thank God) to have definitely improved, everything else is wretched. Just as I foresaw, the Society has lost in you its chief mainstay. Bruchmann, back from his travels, is not the same as he used to be. He seems to cling now to social conventions, and is consequently losing that nimbus which, in my opinion, was due alone to his consistent abstention from all contact with the world. Kupelwieser, as you probably know already, has gone to Rome (but is not particularly pleased with his Russian). What concerns the rest you know better than I.

---

trouble to ask what had happened to his gift, and it was not until forty-one years later that the score was redis- covered and given to the world.

[1] A Private Reading Society (see Letter 34).

[73]

Four individuals have come to fill your and
Kupelwieser's places : namely, the Hungarian
Mayr, Hönig, Smetana, and Steiger ; but
such-like people mostly weaken the Society
instead of strengthening it. What do we want
with a succession of quite ordinary students
and clerks ? If Bruchmann is ill or absent,
one hears by the hour—with Mohn presiding
over all—nothing but endless talk of riding
and fencing, horses and dogs. If it goes on
like this, I shall probably not be able to stand
their company any longer.—

Things are going very badly too with my
two operas. Kupelwieser has suddenly left the
Theatre. Weber's " Euryanthe " was a failure,
and in my opinion its bad reception was
deserved. These circumstances, and a fresh
rupture between Palfy and Barbaja, leave me
with very little hope for my opera. As a
matter of fact it would be no particular blessing [if it were accepted], for everything
nowadays is indescribably badly produced.—

Vogl is here, and has sung once at Bruchmann's, and once at Witzeck's. He interests
himself almost exclusively in my songs. Re-
writes the melodies and makes, so to speak, a
living out of it. For this reason he is extremely
polite and deferent towards me. And now let

us hear something of you. How are you?
Have you already appeared before the public
eye?

Please let me have news of you really soon :
tell me of your life and doings in order to still
in some measure my longing for your presence.
—Since the opera I have composed nothing
except a few more of the Miller-songs. These
will be published in four sets, with vignettes
by Schwind.[1]

I hope I am now in a fair way to recover
my health, and this newly-found blessing will
make me forget many another trouble : but
you, dear Schober, I can never forget, for no one
else can ever be to me, alas, what you once were.

My address :	Your ever-loving
Stubenthor-Bastey,	friend,
No. 1187, on	FRANZ SCHUBERT
the first floor.	

33.   FROM HIS LOST DIARY

25th March, 1824

Sorrow sharpens the understanding and
strengthens the character, whereas happiness

---

[1] The whole Cycle of the " Schöne Müllerin " was
eventually published in five parts, without Schwind's
vignettes, and met at first with a very tepid reception.

seldom troubles about the former, and only makes for weakness or frivolity in the latter.

With all my heart I hate that narrow-mindedness which makes so many wretched people believe that what they think and do is best, and that everything else is worthless. One thing of beauty, it is true, should inspire a man throughout his life, yet the gleam of this single inspiration should illuminate everything else.

27th March

No one to feel the other's grief, no one to understand the other's joy ! People imagine that they can reach one another, but in reality they only pass one another by. Oh misery for him who realizes this !

All that I have created is born of my understanding of music and my own sorrow : that which is engendered by grief alone seems to please the world least of all.

28th March

One step alone divides the sublime from the ridiculous and the greatest wisdom from the grossest stupidity.

Man comes into the world armed with faith,

which is far superior to knowledge and understanding : for in order to understand a thing
one must first of all believe in it. Faith is that
high fundament in which the weaker intellect
erects the first pillars of conviction.

Reason is nothing more than analysed belief.

29th March

O imagination ! Man's greatest treasure,
inexhaustible source at which both Art and
Learning come to drink ! O remain with us,
though recognized and venerated only by the
few, so that we may be safeguarded from so-
called enlightenment, that hideous skeleton
without blood or flesh.

[Undated] 2 o'clock in the night

Enviable Nero ! You were strong enough
to destroy a corrupt people with the sound of
stringed instruments and with song !

34. TO LEOPOLD KUPELWIESER

31st March, 1824

Dear Kupelwieser,

I have been longing to
write to you for a long time past, but could
never hit upon the when and where. Now
comes an opportunity through Smirsch, and
at last I am able to pour out my whole heart

to someone again. You are so good and faithful, you are sure to forgive me things that others would only take very much amiss.— To be brief, I feel myself to be the most unfortunate and the most wretched man in the whole world. Picture to yourself someone whose health is permanently injured, and who, in sheer despair, does everything to make it worse instead of better ; picture to yourself, I say, someone whose most brilliant hopes have come to nothing, someone to whom love and friendship are at most a source of bitterness, someone whose inspiration (whose creative inspiration at least) for all that is beautiful threatens to fail, and then ask yourself if that is not a wretched and unhappy being.

" *Meine Ruh ist hin, mein Herz ist schwer, ich finde sie nimmer und nimmer mehr.*" [1] That could be my daily song now, for every night when I go to sleep I hope never to wake again, and each morning I am only recalled to the griefs of yesterday. So I pass my days, joyless and friendless, except when Schwind comes now and again to see me and brings with him a ray of light from those sweet days that are no more.— Our Society (Reading Society), as you will

---

[1] Gretchen's famous lament in Goethe's " Faust ".

already know, has dealt itself its own death-blow by swelling its ranks with a rowdy chorus of beer-drinkers and sausage-eaters, and it is being dissolved in two days' time—though I myself have scarcely ever attended it since you went away. Leidesdorf, whom I have got to know very well, is a really earnest and good-hearted man, but of such a melancholy disposition that I am afraid his company in this respect may have influenced me rather too much. Things are going badly with him as with me, and ·therefore we never have any money. They declared that it was impossible to make use of your brother's opera,[1]—he made a mistake in leaving the Theatre—and, together with my music, it was not accepted. Castelli's opera " The Conspirators " has been set to music in Berlin by a local composer, and enthusiastically received : so it seems that I have composed two more operas for nothing ! [2] I have written very few new

---

[1] " Fierrabras."

[2] Schubert himself had already written an opera to Castelli's text, and had sent it off to the Management of the Opera House in Vienna. He got the parcel containing his score back a year later—still unopened, and in the meantime the same libretto had been successfully used by a Kapellmeister in Berlin.

songs, but against that I have tried my hand at several kinds of instrumental music and composed two quartets for violins, viola, and violoncello, an octet, and I want to write yet another quartet and so prepare the way for a big symphony.—The latest news in Vienna is that Beethoven is giving a concert, at which his new symphony, three selections from the new Mass, and a new overture will be performed.—I too should like to give a similar concert next year, God willing. I must end now so as not to use up too much paper, and kiss you 1,000 times. If you were to write and tell me about your present mood of inspiration and about the rest of your life, nothing would better please

My address would then be :   Your
c/o Sauer and Leidesdorf's   faithful friend,
music shop, for I am   FRANZ SCHUBERT
going with Esterhazy to   Fare well !
Hungary at the beginning   Right well !
of May.

35. TO HIS BROTHER FERDINAND

Zeléz,
16*th* (*or* 17*th*) *to* 18*th July*, 1824

Beloved Brother,

You can take my word for it that I was really rather hurt at not receiving news either from home or from you for such a long time. Leidesdorf gives no sign of life either, and I wrote to him as well. Do go and look him up in the music shop : he really might send me what I have already written to him about. (You must be really energetic with him though, for he is rather negligent by nature.)[1] You could also find out about the publication of the 3rd set of the " Miller's Songs ". I see nothing in the paper about it. The formation of your quartet astonishes me, and all the more since you have induced Ignaz to join it ! ! ! But it will be better for you to keep to other quartet music than mine, which has nothing to commend it except perhaps that you like it, and you like everything I write. The fact that it reminds you of me is what I treasure most, especially as it does not seem

---

[1] In Schubert's letter this sentence is written as a footnote.

to affect you as much as the waltzes used to at
" The Crown of Hungary ". Was it grief at
my absence alone that drew tears from you,
so that you did not trust yourself to write ?
Or, thinking of me, who am oppressed by
perpetual and incomprehensible longing, did
the same dark veil close about you too ? Or
did all the tears that you have seen me shed
come into your mind again ? Whatever it
was, I feel in this moment more strongly than
ever before that you are my closest friend,
bound to me by every fibre of my being !—
Lest these lines should perhaps lead you
wrongly to suppose that I am not well, or in
poor spirits, let me hasten to assure you of the
contrary. To be sure that blessed time is over
when everything appeared to us in a nimbus
of youthful glory, and we have to face instead
the bitter facts of existence, which I try to
beautify, however, as far as possible with my
own imagination (for which God be thanked !).
One turns instinctively to a place where one
found happiness before, but in vain, for happiness is only to be found within ourselves. In
this way I have met with an unpleasant disappointment, and renewed an experience
already made in Steyr, though I am better
able to find inner peace and happiness now

than I was then.[1]—A long sonata and variations on a theme of my own, both for four hands, which I have already composed, will prove this to you. The variations have met with particular success. I console myself over the songs made over to Mohn, for only a few of them seem to me to be good : for instance, in the lot which contains " The Secret "—the " Wanderer's Night Song " and " Orestes' Atonement ",—yes, not his " abduction " ! That mistake made me laugh very much.[2] Try to get these at any rate back as soon as possible.

Has Kupelwieser not said what he thinks of doing with the opera ? Or where he is sending it ?

Through an oversight I have brought away with me that jackass Hugelthier's quintets (not quartets), and, by God ! he shall not have them

[1] It has been suggested that this particular disappointment had to do with the 17-year-old Countess Caroline Esterhazy. It is known that she inspired in Schubert a hopeless passion, and that one day at Zelez when she asked him in jest why he never dedicated any of his compositions to her, he replied : " Everything I write is dedicated to you anyway ! "

[2] This song seems by an error on the part of the publisher or printer to have been given the title " Der Entführte Orest " (The Abduction of Orestes) by mistake for " Der entsühnte Orest " (The Atonement of Orestes).

back again until he apologizes in words or in writing for his disgusting rudeness. If I get an opportunity, besides, to give this dirty swine a good dressing-down I shall not hesitate to take the fullest advantage of it. But enough of this miserable creature!

That you are so well makes me all the happier in that I hope to enjoy to the uttermost the same good health through the coming winter.

Tenderest remembrances to my parents, brothers and sisters, and friends. A thousand kisses both to you and to your good wife and children. Write as soon as possible, and fare you well, really well ! ! !

N.B. What are Karl and Ignaz doing? They ought to write to me.

With eternal love,

YOUR BROTHER FRANZ

N.B. Has Resi perhaps already presented the world with another citizen ? ? ?

36. TO HELMINA VON CHEZY [1]

Madam,

Convinced as I was of the worth of "Rosamunde" from the first moment of

---

[1] Schubert had written the music for Helmina von Chezy's drama " Rosamunde, Princess of Cyprus " in

reading it, I am very glad that you have undertaken to remove, and I am sure to the best advantage, certain minor defects which only a prejudiced audience could have censured so severely, and I feel especially honoured at receiving a revised copy of the same. As to the fee for the music, I do not think I can fix it at less than 100 Conventional florins, without being derogatory to the music itself. Should this price, however, be too high, I must ask you, Madam, to name one yourself, without diverging too greatly from the amount already suggested, and to have it sent in my absence to the enclosed address.

> With the greatest respect,
> Yours faithfully,
> FRZ. SCHUBERT

Zelez. 5th August, 1824.
Address : Franz Schubert, Teacher at the Schoolhouse in the Rossau in Vienna.

1823. It was given twice, the music being well received. The authoress (" a pleasant poetess but an unbearable woman " according to Weber) found, however, that she must revise the text. In spite of her efforts " Rosamunde " was never performed again.

37. TO MORITZ VON SCHWIND

Zelez,
August, 1824.

Dear Swind,

At last after three months a letter from Schubert, you will say !—It is a long time indeed, but my life here being the simplest possible, I have very little news for you or the others. Indeed, were it not for my longing to know how you and my other special friends are—and above all to hear how things are going with Schober and Kupelwieser—forgive me for saying it, but I might perhaps not have written even now. How is Schober's enterprise succeeding? Is Kupelwieser in Vienna or still in Rome? Is the Reading Society still holding together, or, as I suspect, has it completely broken up? What are you doing??? ———
My good health continues, thank God, and I should be very content here if only I had you, Schober and Kupelwieser with me, but as it is, in spite of the attractive star,[1] I feel at times a desperate longing for Vienna. I hope to see you again at the end of September. I have composed a big sonata and variations for four hands, and the latter have met with a

---

[1] Probably Countess Caroline Esterhazy.

specially good reception here, but I do not entirely trust Hungarian taste, and I shall leave it to you and to the Viennese to decide their true merit.—How is Leidesdorf? Is he making good, or is the dog getting mangy? Please answer all these questions as exactly and as quickly as possible. You have no idea how much I long for a letter from you. And since there is so much for you to tell me, about our friends, about Vienna, and about a thousand other things besides—whereas I have nothing to relate—it really would not have hurt you to have told me some of the news : but perhaps you did not know my address. Before everything else I must ask you to make it a matter of conscience to make a real fuss with Leidesdorf for neither answering my letter nor sending me what I asked him for. What does he mean by it?—the devil take him! The " Miller-songs " are making very slow progress too : a volume comes out every three months. And now good-bye, remember me to anyone you will, and (I repeat) write very soon or else . . .

My address :   Your
Zeléz in Hungary,   true friend,
viâ Raab and Torok,   FRZ. SCHUBERT
c/o Count Joh. Esterhazy
v. Galantha.

38. TO SCHOBER

21st September, 1824

Dear Schober,

I hear that you are not happy? That you have to get over a bad attack of despair? So Swind wrote to me. Although I am exceedingly grieved to hear this, I am not at all surprised, this being the fate of most intelligent people in this miserable world. And, after all, of what use is happiness when the only incitement left to us is misfortune? If only we were together, you, Swind, Kuppel and I, each stroke of ill-luck would be easy enough to bear, but instead we are all separated, each one in a different corner, and in that lies my real unhappiness. I want to cry out with Goethe : " Wer Cringt nur eine Stunde jener holden Zeit Zurück ! " [1] That time when in our intimate circle each showed the other, with motherly diffidence, the children of his Art, and waited, not without apprehension, for the verdict that Love and Truth would pronounce upon them : that time when each inspired the other with a common striving towards the Ideal that

---

[1] "Who will bring back one hour alone of that most blessed time ? "

animated one and all.   Now I am sitting here alone in farthest Hungary, whither I let myself be enticed, alas, for a second time, without a single person near me to whom I can really talk. Since you went away I have written scarcely any songs, but have tried my hand at some instrumental music.   Heaven knows what will happen to my opera ! Although I have been in good health for the past five months, my spirits suffer from your and Kuppel's absence, and I have very wretched days sometimes.   In one of these fits of depression, when the sterility and insignificance that characterize the life of to-day was painfully brought home to me, there came into my head the following lines which I am only showing you because I know that you treat even my weaknesses with love and indulgence.

LAMENT OVER THE NATION

Youth of our time ! Your former power has fled.
The strength of countless nations ebbs away.
None rises up to point a better way.
Valour is lost and inspiration dead.

My days are spent in sorrow's leaden ban,
Sterile and poor, a victim of this age,
Which shrouds in dust our golden heritage,
And brings no greatness unto any man.

[89]

The folk, grown old and feeble, wander by,
Their youthful prowess but a vanished dream,
And even poesy no more esteem,
Its golden glories turn to mockery.

O power of Art ! The sacred task is thine !
Hold up thy mirror to the nobler past !
Thy strength alone can sorrow's strength outlast,
And mock its triumph over our decline.

Up to the time of writing things are going very badly with Leidesdorf. He cannot pay, and no one buys either my things or anybody else's, but only wretched " popular " productions.

I have now informed you pretty exactly how matters stand with me, and I am anxiously awaiting the earliest possible news of your own affairs. The best of all for me would be if you were to come back to Vienna again. I feel confident that you are in good health.

And now good-bye, and write to me as soon as you can.

My address :	Your
Zeléz in Hungary,	SCHUBERT
via Raab and Torok,	Adieu ! ! !
c/o Count Joh. Esterhazy.	

[90]

39. TO GOETHE [1]

Beginning of June, 1825

Your Excellency,

Should I succeed with the dedication of these settings of your poems in expressing my boundless admiration of Your Excellency, and at the same time in earning perhaps something of respect for my unworthy self, the gratification of this wish would be for me the happiest event of my life.

With the greatest respect,

Your most humble servant,

FRANZ SCHUBERT

40. TO JOSEF VON SPAUN

Linz,

21st July, 1825

Dear Spaun,

You can imagine how furious I am at having to write a letter in Linz to you in Lemberg ! ! ! The devil take this in-

---

[1] In June, 1825, Goethe received Schubert's compositions (Goethe Diary, 16th June, 1825, edited by order of the " Grossherzogin Sophie " of Weimar, part III, vol. X, p. 68/28) but never acknowledged them. On the very same day Goethe got quartets from Felix Mendelssohn whom he answered in a rather affectionate and benevolent way.

famous Call of Duty that tears friends so cruelly
apart when they have done no more than sip
at the cup of friendship. Here I am sitting
in Linz, sweating my heart out in this pre-
posterous heat, a full folio of new songs with
me—and you not there ! Are you not ashamed
of yourself? Linz without you is like a body
without a soul, or a horseman without a
head, or soup without salt. Were it not that
Jägermeyr keeps such good beer, and that a
passable wine is to be found on the Schloss-
berg, I should really have to hang myself
on the Promenade, with this superscription :
" Died of grief for the fugitive soul of Linz ! "
As you see, I am treating the rest of Linz
very unfairly, for with your sister, Ottenwald
and Max about me, I am having a very
pleasant time at your mother's house, and your
spirit seems to flash out of the bodies of several
other Linzer folk besides. My only fear is that
this spirit of yours may gradually flicker out,
and then one would burst out of sheer dejection.
It is really distressing how bone-dry and pro-
saic everything in the world is becoming
nowadays, how the majority of people, too,
look on unperturbed at this state of affairs,
and even thrive on it, how comfortably they
slide down through the mire into the abyss.

The upward grade is naturally harder, but the guiding hand of a superior could easily make something even out of this crowd. For the rest, do not let the fact that you are so far away from us make you grey-headed. Defy the foolish fate that has taken you there, and prove your scorn by letting your fertile fancies blossom like a flower garden : show your divine descent, and diffuse life-giving warmth throughout the frozen North. Base is the grief that makes a high heart falter ! Away with it, and trample underfoot before it is too late the vulture that gnaws at your vitals.

Some very strange, one might almost say comical, notices have appeared about Schober. First of all I read in the Viennese *Theaterzeitung* about a pseudonymous " Torupsohn " ? ? ? ? [1] What can that mean ? He surely cannot have married ? That would be really rather amusing ! Secondly, that his best rôle is that of the clown in the travesty of " Aline ". Rather a mighty fall from all his high expectations and plans ! And thirdly and lastly, that he may be returning to Vienna. I wonder what he will do there ? Meanwhile

---

[1] Schober's birthplace was the castle of Torup near Malmö in Sweden.

I am looking forward very much to seeing him again, and hope that he will enrich once more our sadly depleted society with a livelier and wiser being. I have been in Upper Austria since May 20th, and was very vexed to hear that you had left Linz a few days earlier. I should have liked so much to see you once again before the devil took you to . . . Poland. I only stayed fourteen days in Steyer, and then we (Vogl and I) went on to Gmunden where we spent very pleasantly six whole weeks. We lodged with Traweger, who possesses a splendid pianoforte and is, as you know, a great admirer of my humble self. My life there was delightfully free and easy. There was frequent music at Hofrat von Schiller's, and amongst other things some of my new songs from Walter Scott's "Lady of the Lake" were heard, the "Hymn to the Virgin Mary" in particular being generally approved. I am very glad that you are seeing something of young Mozart. Remember me to him. And now good-bye! My dear old Spaun! Think often of

Your sincere friend,
FRANZ SCHUBERT

N.B. Do write to me
    at Steyer.

41.   TO HIS FATHER AND STEPMOTHER

Steyer,
25*th July,* 1825

Dearest Parents,

I justly deserve your re-
proach for my long silence, but as the present
time offers very little of interest and I dislike
writing empty phrases, you must forgive me for
not giving an account of myself until I had
your dear letter.   I am very glad to hear that
you are one and all in good health and, God
be praised, I can now say the same.   I am back
again in Steyer, but was six weeks in Gmunden, where the surrounding country, which is
heavenly, touched me very deeply—as did also
the inhabitants, particularly the good Traweger
—and did me a world of good. I was
absolutely free at Traweger's, just as though I
were at home.   Later on, after the appearance
of Herr Hofrat von Schiller, who is monarch of
the whole Salzkammergut, we (Vogl and I) had
our meals every day at his house, and played
both there and also very frequently at
Traweger's. My new songs from Walter
Scott's " Lady of the Lake " in particular had
a great success.   There was a good deal of
surprise too at my piety, which found ex-

pression in a Hymn to the Blessed Virgin, which seems to have moved all hearts and created quite a devotional atmosphere. I fancy that is because my religious feeling is never forced, and I never compose hymns or prayers of this sort unless I am involuntarily overcome by a sense of devotion, and then the feeling is, as a rule, genuine and heartfelt. From Gmunden we went by way of Pusch-berg, where we met several acquaintances and stopped a few days, and so to Linz where we spent eight days, partly in Linz itself and partly in Steyereck. In Linz I lodged at the Spauns' house, where they are still very sad at Spaun (the one you know) being transferred to Lem-berg. I read several letters, all very depressed and betraying obvious home-sickness, which he had written from Lemberg. I wrote to him and pulled him up sharply for his weakness, though, were I in his place, I suspect I should be even more miserable than he. In Steyreck we stayed with Countess Weissenwolf, who is a great admirer of my humble self, possesses everything I have written, and sings many of the things very prettily too. The Walter Scott songs made such an extremely good im-pression on her that she made it clear that she would be by no means displeased were

I to dedicate them to herself. But in connection with these I mean to break with the usual publishing procedure, which brings in so little profit. I feel that these songs, bearing as they do the celebrated name of Scott, are likely to arouse more curiosity, and—if I add the English text—should make my name better known in England too. If only honest dealing were possible with these . . . publishers : but the wise and beneficent regulations of our Government have taken good care that the artist shall remain the eternal slave of these miserable money-grabbers.

With regard to the letter from Milder, I am very pleased about the good reception accorded to " Suleika ", though I wish I could have had a look at the *critique* myself to see if there were anything to be learnt from it. A review, however favourable, can be at the same time ridiculous, if the critic lacks reasonable intelligence, as is not seldom the case.

I have come across my compositions all over Upper Austria, but especially in the monasteries at St. Florian and at Kremsmünster, where, assisted by an excellent pianist, I gave a very successful recital of my Variations and Marches for four hands. The Variations from my new Sonata for two hands met with special

G

enthusiasm. These I played alone, and not unsuccessfully, for several people assured me that under my fingers the keys were transformed into singing voices : which, if it be true, pleases me very much, as I cannot abide that cursed hacking of the instrument to which even first-class pianists are addicted : it pleases neither the ear nor the heart. I am back in Steyer now, and should you wish to cheer me with a quick letter, it would still reach me here, for we shall stop another 10 to 14 days, and then set out for Gastein, one of the most famous watering-places, about 3 days' journey from Steyer. I am looking forward extremely to this journey, for in this way I shall get to know the most beautiful districts, and on the way back we shall visit Salzburg too, which is renowned for its splendid position and surrounding country. We shall not get back from this expedition before the middle of September, and have then promised to re-visit Gmunden, Linz, Steyereck, and [St.] Florian, so I shall hardly get to Vienna before the end of October. Will you therefore engage me my old rooms near the Karlskirche, and also please pay 28 Viennese florins for them, which sum I will gratefully refund you on arrival, for I have promised it already, and it is quite possible that I may get back earlier than I thought. Throughout the whole of June and during half July the weather was very unsettled, then for 14 days it was so hot that I got quite thin, merely from perspiring so much, and now it has rained for 4 days practically without ceasing. My best greetings to Ferdinand and his wife and children. He is still biting the dust and all his resolutions to get away from Dornbach seem to have failed. I am certain that he has been ill 77 times again, and fancied himself 9 times at least on the point of death —as though dying were the worst evil we mortals had to face. If only he could see these marvellous mountains and lakes, whose aspect threatens to crush us or swallow us up, he would become less enamoured of the tiny span of human life, and would be ready joyfully to give his body to the earth, to be quickened by its incomprehensible forces into new life. What is Karl doing ? Will he leave home or not ? He must have plenty to do nowadays, for a married artist is obliged to produce both works of Art and works of Nature, and when both kinds are successful he is to be doubly congratulated, for that is no trifling perform-ance ! It is not for me ! Ignaz is, I expect, with Hollpein just now, for as he is there morning, noon and night, he will hardly be at home. I cannot refrain from admiring his perseverance, though I am not at all sure if it be a merit or otherwise, nor whether he is the more deserving thereby of Heaven or Hell. He really might enlighten me about that. The Schneider and his Schneiderin [1] must take great care of the little he- or she-Schneider now on the way. May the race of Schneiders become as innumerable as the sands of the sea ! Only they must see to it that there are no braggarts (Aufschneider) or cutters (Zuschneider) or defamers (Ehrenabschneider) or cut-throats (Gurgelabschneider) amongst them ! And now I must put an end at last to all this prattle : I felt, you see, that I must make up for my long silence with an equally long letter. A thousand kisses to Marie and Pepi and little André Probst. Indeed, I must beg you to give my heartiest greetings to everyone possible. Hoping for an answer soon, I remain, with all love,   Your

faithful son

FRANZ

---

[1] Schubert's sister and brother-in-law. The whole passage is a play on their name Schneider (" tailor ").

42. TO HIS BROTHER FERDINAND

Gmunden,
12*th September,* 1825

Dear Brother,

Since you have begged me to do so, of course I should like to give you a detailed account of our journey to Salzburg and Gastein, though you know what a poor hand I am at relating and describing things. However, as I should have to do this in any case on getting back to Vienna, I would prefer to give you in writing now rather than in words later a faint idea of all this extraordinary beauty, for I feel this way is likely to be more successful than the other.

We set out then from Steyer about the middle of August, and went by way of Kremsmünster, which indeed I had often seen before, but which, on account of its fine position, I can never pass by. You look right over a very lovely valley, broken here and there by gentle hillocks, to the right of which rises a fair-sized hill, and from the road that leads down from it—over a brook running in the contrary direction—you have a magnificent view of the great monastery spread out along the hill's crest, and of the extremely picturesque Mathematical

Tower.[1] We met with a very friendly reception, being already well known here, especially Herr von Vogl, who was educated at the monastery. We did not stop, however, but continued our journey, which does not call for any particular comment, as far as Vöklabruk, which we reached that night : a dismal little hole. Next morning we came by way of Strasswalchen and Frankenmarkt to Neumarkt, where we had our midday meal. These villages, which lie in the territory of Salzburg, are remarkable for the peculiar construction of their houses. Nearly everything is of wood. The wooden kitchen utensils rest on wooden stands, and these are placed outside the houses, round which run wooden balconies. Old targets too, pierced through and through, are to be found hanging up everywhere outside the houses. These are preserved as trophies of victory from a long time past : the dates 1600 and 1500 are frequently to be found on them. Here already circulates the Bavarian money. From Neumarkt, the last post-relay before Salzburg, mountain peaks with fresh snow upon them were already visible, rising

---

[1] So called from the collection of mathematical and astronomical instruments which it contains.

out of the Salzburg valley. About an hour or
so from Neumarkt the country becomes really
fine. The Waller lake's clear blue-green
stretch of water gives a vivid touch of colour
to this wholly charming landscape. The land
here lies very high, and from this point the
road drops steadily down as far as Salzburg.
The mountains rise up ever higher, in
particular the Untersberg, which stands out,
fantastic and wonderful, above the rest. The
villages show traces of former prosperity.
Marble window-frames and door-posts are to
be found everywhere, even in the poorest farm-
houses, and sometimes staircases of red marble
too. The sun grows dim, and heavy clouds
like the spirits of the mist float over the black
mountains. Yet they do not touch the summit
of the Untersberg, but creep past it, as though
fearful of its ghostly secret.[1] The broad valley
with its sprinkling of solitary castles, churches
and farmyards, slowly unfolds itself before our
spellbound eyes. Towers and palaces gradually appear, and at last we pass the Kapuziner-
berg, whose vast wall of rock rises sheer up

[1] According to legend Charlemagne and his paladins
are biding their time in the Untersberg until, one day,
they ride out in state to bring Germany to its former
greatness and splendour.

from the roadway, and frowns menacingly down upon the traveller below. The Untersberg and its attendant mountains assume gigantic proportions, as though they would crush us with their magnitude. And now the road leads by way of some very fine avenues into the town itself. This famous Seat of the former Electors is surrounded by fortresses built of great blocks of freestone. The inscriptions on the city gates bear witness to the vanished power of the Church. The moderately broad streets are filled with houses all five or six stories high, and our way now lies, past the quaintly decorated house of Theophrastus Paracelsus,[1] over the bridge which spans the dark and foaming torrent of the Salzach. The town itself made rather a gloomy impression upon me, for the bad weather caused the ancient buildings to look more sombre still, and the fortress which stands on the highest peak of the Mönchberg seems to send its ghostly greeting down through every street. Unfortunately just after our arrival the rain set in—no rare event here—and our sight-seeing in consequence was confined to the many

---

[1] One of the most famous doctors of the sixteenth century.

[104]

palaces and splendid churches which we had already glimpsed in driving past. Through Herr Pauernfeind, a merchant known to Herr von Vogl, we obtained an introduction to Count Platz, President of the Provincial Estates, whose family, being already acquainted with our names, received us with all possible kindness. Vogl sang some of my songs, whereupon we received a pressing invitation to perform the seven items of our programme again before a specially chosen audience on the following evening. On this occasion the Ave Maria mentioned in my first letter met with particular favour and touched all hearts. The way in which Vogl sings and I accompany him, so that we seem to be fused for the moment into a single being, is something entirely new and unknown to these people. Next morning, after climbing the Mönchberg, from which there is a view over the greater part of the town, I was really astonished at the quantity of splendid buildings, palaces and churches. Yet the number of inhabitants here is small : many of the buildings stand empty, several are only occupied by one, or at the most, two or three families. In the many beautiful squares grass grows between the paving-stones—so few people pass through them.

The cathedral is a heavenly building, on the pattern of St. Peter's in Rome, but of course on a smaller scale. The church is in the form of a Cross, and is surrounded by four vast courtyards, each of which forms in itself a public square. Colossal figures of the Apostles, carved in stone, stand at the entrance doors. The interior of the church rests on a number of marble pillars, is adorned with portraits of the Electors, and is really beautiful in every part. The light, which shines in through the cupola, illuminates every corner. The effect produced by this extraordinary clarity is most wonderful, and all other churches would do well to imitate it. In the four courtyards about the church there are great fountains, and these are decorated with the finest and boldest figures imaginable. From here we went into St. Peter's monastery, where Michael Haydn [1] once lived. This church is wonderful too. Here too, as you know, is M. Haydn's monument. It is handsome enough, but badly placed in a remote corner, and the scraps of

---

[1] Brother of the more famous Joseph. He spent practically his whole life in Salzburg, first as conductor to the Cardinal Archbishop's private orchestra, and later as organist to the cathedral. He is best known as a composer of church music.

music-paper carved round it make rather a silly
effect. The urn contains his head. I thought
to myself : May your calm, clear spirit, good
Haydn, rest upon me, and though I cannot
ever be so quiet and so clear, yet certainly no
one on earth reveres you more than I ! (A slow
tear fell from my eyes, and we went on further.)
We had our midday meal at Herr Pauernfeind's, and in the afternoon, as the weather
allowed us to get out, we climbed the Nonnen-
berg, which though not very high, has the most
beautiful view of all. You see right over the
Vale of Salzburg spread out behind. It is
almost impossible to give you any idea of the
loveliness of this valley. You must imagine
to yourself a garden, many miles in circum-
ference, in which innumerable castles and
estates peer out through or above the trees.
Imagine a river too, winding its serpentine
course through ; meadows and fields like so
many exquisitely coloured carpets ; excellent
roads which twist ribbon-like about them ;
and finally vast avenues of gigantic trees : all
this surrounded by an immense range of mountains, as though they were the guardians of this
heavenly valley. Imagine all this and you will
have a faint idea of its unspeakable beauty.
The rest of our sight-seeing in Salzburg will

only be done on the return journey, and I
will leave it till then, for I want to continue
my description in the right chronological order.

43. TO JOHANN STEIGER VON AMSTEIN

Gmunden,
Middle of September, 1825

Dear Steiger,

I am very sorry that I cannot
accompany you to Clodi. But we are going
to the Atter lake to-day, and this expedition
cannot be put off, for Vogl has made up his
mind to leave Gmunden to-morrow !! I was
only told early this morning, so I am sure
you will forgive me. Please do not be vexed,
for I am really very sorry. I hope to see
you all once more at your usual Inn this
evening.

With regard to visiting the salt-mines, you
should ask at Kuffner's office for Herr von
Kinesberger, who spoke to us yesterday.

Your

SCHUBERT

44. TO EDUARD VON BAUERNFELD

Steyer,
18*th or* 19*th September,* 1825

Dear friend,
Your scribble had slipped in-
deed right out of my mind ! All-destroying
Time and your own unconscionably hasty hand-
writing have brought things to this pass !
As regards the last, I propose to pay you back
in your own coin.—As to my quarters in
Frühwirth's house, I mean to keep them on,
and have already tried through my people
at home to let him know this, but it seems
that they have forgotten to do so, or else
he is being over-anxious and fussy. In any
case would you be so good, either singly or
collectively, to pay him 25 Viennese florins
on my behalf, and to assure him that I shall
be back without fail at the end of October.—
As to setting up house together, I should
be pleased enough to do so, but I know these
bachelor- and student-plans only too well,
and do not want in the end to fall between
two stools. Should anything suitable turn up
in the meantime I could always find some good
excuse for parting on friendly terms with my
present landlord. The 25 florins mentioned

[109]

above should be handed over to him for
October, and on my arrival I will pay them
back without delay.—I am very eager to meet
Schober and Kuppelwieser and see how a
man looks (*a*) when all his plans have ended
in smoke, and (*b*) when he has just come
back from Rome and Naples.—Schwind is a
dithering wool-gatherer. Of the two letters
he wrote me each is more muddle-headed
than the other. Such a grotesque mixture
of sense and nonsense has never come my
way before. Unless he has done some really
fine work during this time, such brainless
chatter is not to be forgiven him. Give
greetings to all three and also to Rieder and
Dietrich if you see them. My congratulations to Rieder on his professorship.—Steiger
and Louis Hönig came to see me in Gmunden,
which pleased me very much. If only your
otherwise excellent brains had reached just a
little farther, the idea of honouring me with
your presence would have occurred to you
too. But that is asking too much of lads as
head-over-ears in love as you all are. How
often, I wonder, have you been reduced to
fresh despair, and had to drown your sighs
and lamentations in beer and punch ! Ha !
ha ! ha ! ha ! I nearly forgot to tell you

that I have been in Salzburg and Gastein, where the country surpasses the wildest flights of fancy.

Good-bye!

Your

SCHUBERT

Write to me, but something sensible—say a musical poem. (?)!

Greetings to all my friends.

N.B. Vogl has just told me that he may possibly be going to Italy with Haugwitz at the end of this month or the beginning of October. In that case I should be back earlier, at the beginning of October.

45. TO HIS BROTHER FERDINAND

[Continuation of the letter dated
12th September]

Steyer,
21st September

From the date above you will see that several days have slipped by between these lines and my last, and that we have moved, alas! from Gmunden to Steyer. So to continue the account of our journey—(which I may say I now regret ever having begun, since it runs away with so much of my

[111]

time !)—what followed was so to say as
follows : the following day, namely, was the
loveliest in the whole world. The Untersberg [1] or rather, highest mountain, with its
own squadron and the rest of the mountainous
mob, shone and sparkled magnificently in—
or rather close to—the sun. We drove through
the valley already described as through Ely-
sium, though our paradise had this advantage
over the other, that we were seated in a
delightfully comfortable carriage, a luxury
unknown to Adam and Eve. Instead of
encountering wild beasts we met with many a
charming girl. . . . It is really not right to
make such feeble jokes in such beautiful sur-
roundings, but I simply cannot be serious
to-day. Thus, sunk in bliss, we steered our
easy course through the lovely day and still
lovelier country, until our attention was
caught by an attractive building known as
Monat-Schlösschen because an Elector had
it built in a single month for a fair lady.
Everyone here knows this, but no one is
shocked. What enchanting tolerance ! The
charm of this little building certainly adds to
the beauty of the valley. A few hours later
we came into the remarkable but extremely

---

[1] I.e. " lower mountain ".

dirty and dismal town of Hallein. The
inhabitants all look like ghosts : pale, hollow-
eyed, and thin as sticks. The dreadful con-
trast between this wretched townlet [1] and the
surrounding valley made the gloomiest impression upon me. It was like falling from
heaven on to a dung-heap, or hearing, after
Mozart's music, some piece by the immortal
A. Vogl was not to be persuaded to see
either the salt mountain or the salt-mines,
for his great soul, harried by gout, pressed
forward to Gastein alone, as a traveller in the
dark towards a point of light. So we drove
on further past Golling, where the first un-
scaleable mountains came into view, whose
fearful gorges are crossed by the Lueg Pass.
After we had crawled slowly up the side of
one great mountain, with other terrible ones
to either side and just in front of us—as
though the whole world were boarded up
here, and no possible way through—having
reached the highest point, we looked suddenly
sheer down into a terrifying ravine, and my
heart leapt to my throat. After we had re-

---

[1] Schubert uses the word " Ratzenstadtl " (" Rats-
town "). He probably was reminded of the poorest
quarter of Vienna, which bore this name.

H

covered a little from the first shock, we were able to look at the fantastically high walls of rock which seemed to end some distance away in a blind alley with no visible outlet. In the midst of these fearful works of Nature, man has striven to immortalize his still more fearful bestiality. For here, where far, far below the Salzach foams and thunders over its rocky bed, there took place that fearful massacre of the Bavarians on one side of the river by the Tyrolese on the other. The Tyrolese, concealed on the rocky heights, fired down with fiendish and triumphant yells on to the Bavarians who were trying to gain the Pass, and those who were hit were precipitated into the abyss, without so much as seeing whence the shots came. A chapel was erected on the Bavarian side, and a red Cross set up in the rocks on the Tyrolean side, partly to commemorate this extremely shameful outbreak which continued for several days and weeks, and partly as an act of expiation. O glorious Christ, to how many deeds of shame must Thou lend Thine image! They set up Thy likeness—Who art Thyself the most terrible monument of all to man's fallen state!—as though to say, Behold! We have trampled with impious feet upon Almighty

God's most perfect creation. Would one scruple then to destroy with a light heart the remainder of this vermin known as man? But let us turn away our eyes from such melancholy sights, and apply ourselves rather to finding a way out of this hole. After we had dropped down for a considerable time, with both walls of rock drawing ever closer together, and the road and stream narrowing down to a total breadth of just 2 *klafters* across, under a projecting crag, at a point where the Salzach rages furiously at its narrow bonds, the main road appeared where least it was expected, to the travellers' pleasant surprise. Though still shut in by mountains as high as the sky, the road now continued broad and level. In the afternoon we came to Werffen, a market town with an important fortress that was built by the Electors of Salzburg and is now being restored by the Emperor. On the way back we climbed up to it. It is d[amnably] high, but offers a splendid view over the valley, which is bounded on one side by the immense range of the Werffen mountains. These are visible as far as Gastein. Heavens! Hell! Describing a journey is a terrible business. I simply cannot do any more. As I shall be coming back to Vienna

in any case at the beginning of October, I
will hand over this scrawl to you then myself,
and tell you the rest in words.

46. TO THE EMPEROR FRANCIS II

Your Majesty !
Most gracious Emperor !

        With the deepest
submission the undersigned humbly begs Your
Majesty graciously to bestow upon him the
vacant position of Vice-Kapellmeister to the
Court, and supports his application with the
following qualifications :

(1) The undersigned was born in Vienna, is
the son of a school-teacher, and is 29 years of age.

(2) He enjoyed the privilege of being for
five years a Court Chorister at the Imperial
and Royal College School.

(3) He received a complete course of instruc-
tion in Composition from the late Chief
Kapellmeister to the Court, Herr Anton Salieri,
and is fully qualified, therefore, to fill any
post as Kapellmeister. (See Appendix A.) [1]

---

[1] This was a testimonial from Salieri, who had died in
May, 1825. Schubert had no influential friends to speak
for him at Court, and after a year's delay the post was
given to someone else.

(4) His name is well known, not only in Vienna but throughout Germany, as a composer of songs and instrumental music.

(5) He has also written and arranged five Masses for both smaller and larger orchestras, and these have already been performed in various churches in Vienna.

(6) Finally, he is at the present time without employment, and hopes in the security of a permanent position to be able to realize at last those high musical aspirations which he has ever kept before him.

Should Your Majesty be graciously pleased to grant this request, the undersigned would strive to the utmost to give full satisfaction.

Your Majesty's most obedient humble servant,

FRANZ SCHUBERT

Vienna. 7th April, 1826.

[Outside :]

To His Most Gracious Majesty the Emperor.

[Below :]

Franz Schubert, Composer in Vienna, humbly presents his petition for nomination to the vacant post of Vice-Kapellmeister to the Court. Resident at No. 100 Auf der Wieden, close to the Karlskirche, 5th staircase, 2nd floor.

47. TO BAUERNFELD AND FERDINAND VON MAYERHOFER

[*Vienna,
Beginning of May,* 1826]

Dear Bauernfeld,
Dear Mayrhofer,

That you have written the opera text is an excellent move, and I only wish that I had it before me now. They have asked for my operas to see if anything could be done with them, and if only your libretto were ready I could submit this to them instead, and as soon as its worth was recognized—about which I have no doubts— why then in Heaven's name one could get to work on it, or else send it to Milder in Berlin. Mlle Schechner has made her appearance here in the " Swiss Family ", and was very enthusiastically received. In some ways she is very like Milder and on that account should be popular with us here.—Do not stay away too long. Everything here is very miserable and depressing. The general tediousness of life has already gained too strong a hold upon us. Schober and Schwind give vent only to lamentations that are far more heartrending than those we listened to during Holy Week. Since you left I have scarcely been to Grinzing

once, and never with Schwind. . . . From all
this you can deduce a fine sum-total of gaiety!
" The Magic Flute " was very well produced
at the Theatre an der Wien; " Der Frei-
schütz " at the Imperial and Royal Kärnt-
nertor Theatre very badly. Herr Jacob and
Frau Baberl at the Leopoldstadt Theatre are un-
surpassed. Your poem which appeared in the
Modezeitung is very good, but the one in your
last letter is finer still. Its sublime humour
and comic loftiness of sentiment, and especially
the gentle cry of anguish at the end, where
you take advantage in a masterly fashion—
oh, yes indeed !—of the good town of Villach,
place it among the finest examples of its kind.—
I am not working at all.—The weather here
is really terrible, and the Almighty seems to
have forsaken us entirely. The sun refuses to
shine. It is already May, and one cannot
even sit in the garden. Fearful! Dreadful!!
Appalling !!! For me the greatest cruelty
one can imagine. In June Schwind and I
want to go with Spaun to Linz. We might
all arrange to meet there or in Gmunden,
only you must let us know definitely and as
soon as possible if you could manage it. Not
in two months' time !

    Good-bye !

48. TO FRANZ SALES KANDLER

Dear Sir,

Would you be so good as to have my Mass, which is now in your possession, sent either to the publisher Herr Leidesdorf or to Messrs. Pennauer?

Yours faithfully,

FRZ. SCHUBERT

Vienna 30th June, 1826.

49. TO HANS GEORG NÄGELI IN ZÜRICH

Vienna,
4th July, 1826

Dear Sir,

My Sonata in A minor made you no doubt better acquainted with me, since you have now done me the honour of commissioning, through Herr Carl Czerny, a Pianoforte Sonata which you propose to include in a collection of similar compositions (under the title : Ehrenpforte). The good reception which you have been kind enough to accord to my Sonata and, above all, your extremely flattering demand, make me very willing to comply with this request without delay.

In that case I must request you to make

the fee of 120 Conventional florins[1] payable in advance to me in Vienna.

Let me add how gratifying it is to me to be in correspondence with such an old-established and famous publishing house.

With the greatest respect, I remain
Yours faithfully,
FRANZ SCHUBERT

My address is :

Auf der Wieden, No. 100, in Frühwirth's house, 5th staircase, 2nd floor

50.   TO BAUERNFELD

Vienna,
10*th July,* 1826

Dear Bauernfeld,

It is impossible for me to come either to Gmunden or anywhere else, for I have absolutely no money, and everything else is going very badly with me too.   However, I am bearing up, and am in good spirits.

Do come back to Vienna as soon as you can. Duport wants me to write an opera for him, but he does not like any of the texts which I have already used, so it would be really splendid if your opera-libretto were accepted.

---

[1] About £12.

Schwind has quite lost his head as regards Nettel.[1] Schober is now in trade. Vogl is married ! ! !

Please come as soon as you possibly can ! On account of the opera. You have only to mention my name in Linz, and you   Your will be well looked after.   SCHUBERT

51.   TO THE PUBLISHERS BREITKOPF AND HÄRTEL
IN LEIPZIG

Vienna,
12*th August*, 1826

Dear Sirs,

In the hope that my name is not wholly unknown to you, I am venturing to ask whether you would be disposed to take over at a moderate price some of my compositions, for I very much want to become as well known as possible in Germany. Your selection could be made from the following :— songs with pianoforte accompaniment, string

---

[1] Schwind was in love with Annette Hönig, but their engagement was broken off later.   According to Bauernfeld, the bridegroom could not tolerate the philistine outlook of the Hönig family, and they on their side disapproved of his Bohemian life and " lack of piety ".

quartets, pianoforte sonatas, pieces for four hands, etc., etc., and I have also written an octet. Should you avail yourselves of this suggestion I should feel it a special honour to be associated with such an old-established and well-known publishing house.

Awaiting an early reply,

I remain, with the greatest respect,

Yours faithfully,

FRANZ SCHUBERT

My address :

Auf der Wieden,

No. 100, close to the Karlskirche, 5th staircase, 2nd floor.

52. TO H. A. PROBST IN LEIPZIG

Vienna,

12 *August* 1826

Dear Sir,

In the hope that my name is not entirely unknown to you I beg to put forward the proposal, which I trust may meet with your approval, that you should take over some of my compositions for a moderate fee, since I am anxious to become as well known as possible in Germany. The choice at your disposal in-

[123]

cludes songs with pianoforte accompaniment, string quartets, sonatas for the pianoforte, pieces for four hands, etc etc. I have also written an octet for 2 violins, viola, violoncello, double-bass, clarinet, bassoon and horn. In any case I esteem it an honour to be in correspondence with you. Hoping for an early reply,

> I remain,
> with all respect,
> yours faithfully,
> FRANZ SCHUBERT

My address : Auf der Wieden No. 100, next door to the Karlskirche, 5th staircase, 2nd floor.

53. **TO THE GESELLSCHAFT DER MUSIKFREUNDE**

Vienna,
Beginning of October, 1826

To the Executive of the Austrian Musical Society.

Convinced as I am of the noble aim of the Austrian Musical Society to give whole-hearted support to every effort made in the cause of Art, I venture now, as an Austrian musician,

to dedicate to, and commend to the good care
of, the Society, this Symphony of mine.[1]

> With the greatest respect,
> Yours faithfully,
> FRZ. SCHUBERT

54. TO IGNAZ VON SEYFRIED

Dear Sir,

Please be so good as to let me
know by the bearer of this whether my overture
to " Rosamunde " has been found. Otherwise
I should find myself in a terrible position, for
it is supposed to be given on the 2nd December.[2]

So, once again, I beg you to let me have
word as soon as possible.

> I remain, with all respect,
> Yours faithfully,
> FRZ. SCHUBERT

Vienna. 23rd December, 1826

55. TO THE GESELLSCHAFT DER MUSIKFREUNDE

The Executive Committee of the Society
of the Friends of Music in the Empire of

---

[1] The Society took such " good care " of the " Gastein
Symphony " that it disappeared and has never been
found since.

[2] No doubt " January " is meant.

Austria having found me worthy of election
to their representative body, I beg to record
my gratification at the honour accorded to me
by this election, and my entire readiness to
fulfil all obligations connected with the same.

FRANZ SCHUBERT
Composer

Vienna. 12*th June,* 1827.

56. TO MARIE LEOPOLDINE PACHLER IN GRAZ

Vienna,
12*th June,* 1827.

Honoured and gracious Lady,

Though I fail
to see how I come to deserve such a friendly
offer as that which you have made me in
your letter to Jenger, and doubt indeed if I
shall ever be able to repay it in any way,
yet I cannot but accept an invitation which
gives me an opportunity, not only of seeing
at last the much-praised town of Grätz,
but also of becoming personally acquainted,
Madam, with yourself.

I remain, Madam,

with the greatest respect,

Yours faithfully,
FRZ. SCHUBERT

57. TO FRANZ SELLIERS DE MORANVILLE

Dear Herr von Sellier,

        I came to apologize for not having kept to my word the other day. If you only knew how impossible it was for me to do so, I am sure you would forgive me. Hoping that I may not forfeit your friendly esteem thereby,

  I remain with the greatest respect,
        Yours faithfully,
          FRZ. SCHUBERT

Grätz. 19th September, 1827.

58. TO MARIE LEOPOLDINE PACHLER

Vienna,
27th September, 1827

Dear Madam,

       I realize now that my life in Grätz was far too pleasant, and I am finding it very hard to settle down in Vienna again. It is big enough, to be sure, but on the other hand it is devoid of open-heartedness and sincerity, of genuine ideas and sensible talk, and, above all, of intellectual accomplishments. There is such a perpetual babel of small-talk

[127]

here, that it is difficult to know if one has a head on one's shoulders or not, and one rarely or never attains to any inward happiness. Though I daresay that, to a great extent, is my own fault, for I take so long to come out of my shell. I soon recognized the unaffected sincerity of social life in Grätz, and, had my visit been longer, I should have got into the way of it still more. In particular I shall never forget the friendly hospitality accorded to me or your good self or the sturdy Pachleros or little Faust, for with you I spent the happiest days I have known for a long time. Hoping to find some adequate way of expressing my gratitude,

I remain,
Yours most sincerely,

FRZ. SCHUBERT

N.B. I hope to be able to send the opera libretto in a few days' time.

59. TO THE SAME

I enclose herewith, dear Madam, the four-handed piece for little Faust. I am afraid, however, that it may not meet with his approval, for I do not feel myself particularly suited to compositions of this sort. I hope that you, Madam, are enjoying better health than I, for my usual headaches have come back again. I beg to send my heartiest congratulations to Doctor Karl for his nameday festivities, and to say that I have not yet been able to get back the libretto for my opera from that lazy beast, Herr Gottdank, who has kept it to read through for months now.

    With the greatest respect,
I remain,
Yours most sincerely,
FRANZ SCHUBERT

Vienna. 12*th October*, 1827.

60. TO JOHANN PHILIPP NEUMANN

Vienna,
16*th October*, 1827

Dear Herr Professor,
I have duly received

the 100 Viennese florins which you sent me for composing the hymns for the Mass, and I only hope that these compositions may fulfil all your expectations.

    With the greatest respect I remain,
Yours faithfully,
FRANZ SCHUBERT

[129]

61. TO JOHANN BAPTIST JENGER

7 November, 1827

Dear Friend,

Please forgive me, but I cannot come to dinner at midday to-day at Henikstein's. I will turn up however without fail in the evening at half-past 7.

SCHUBERT

62. TO THE SAME

[? 1827]

Dear Jenger,

Forgive me. I cannot come to dinner. We shall meet at half-past 7 to-night.

SCHUBERT

63. TO JOHANN FRIEDRICH ROCHLITZ [1]

Vienna,
November (?), 1827

Dear Sir,

I was much honoured by your letter in as much as it was a means of bringing

---

[1] Weber had already set this poem to music, but Councillor Rochlitz was not satisfied with the result, and tried to win Beethoven's interest. When this failed he turned to Schubert, whose reward was to be " as perfect a performance as possible " in Leipzig. Schubert's reply was not very enthusiastic, and the project fell through.

me into closer touch with a most distinguished man.

I have given considerable thought to your proposal regarding the poem " The First Tone ", and I feel that your suggested treatment of it might indeed produce a very fine effect. As, however, it is more of a melodrama [1] than an oratorio or cantata, and the former (perhaps rightly) is no longer popular, I must frankly confess that I should greatly prefer a poetical work that could be treated as an oratorio, partly because it is not always possible to find a man like Anschütz to declaim, but also because it is my greatest wish to produce a musical work with no other aid than the inspiration of a long poem of a type that essentially lends itself to a musical setting. I think I must not tell you that I am thinking you to be the real poet for a song like that and certainly I would do my best setting it to music.

" The First Tone " is in any case a splendid poem, and should you really wish me to set it to music, I would endeavour to do so, though, with your consent, I would arrange

---

[1] "Melodrama" in this connection means declamation with instrumental accompaniment.

for the music (the actual singing, that is) to begin at the words : " *Then I perceived* ".

With the expression of my greatest respect,

Yours faithfully,

FRZ. SCHUBERT.

64. TO ANSELM HÜTTENBRENNER

Vienna,
18*th January*, 1828

My dear old Hüttenbrenner ! ! !

Are you surprised at my writing after all this time ? I am myself ! But there is a good reason for it now. So listen ! At your end in Grätz a drawing-master's post has fallen vacant, and candidates for the same have already been requested to send in their nomination papers. My brother Carl, whom I think you also know, wants to obtain this post. He is highly skilled, both as a landscape painter and also as a draughtsman. If you could manage to do something for him in this affair, I should be infinitely grateful. You are an influential man in Grätz, and maybe you know someone either in the Government or elsewhere who has a voice in the matter.—My brother is married and has children, and he would be very

[132]

glad, therefore, to find himself in an assured position. I hope that all goes well with you, and with your dear family and brothers too. My warmest greetings to them all. A trio of mine for pianoforte, violin and violoncello was given at Schuppanzigh's house the other day, and pleased everyone very much. Boklet, Schuppanzigh[1] and Linke played it admirably. Have you written nothing new? Apropos, why does not Greiner, or whatever his name is, publish your two songs? What the devil is the meaning of it?

I repeat my request made above. Remember that whatever you do for my brother you are doing for me.

Hoping for a favourable reply,
     I remain
        till death
        your faithful friend,
             FRZ. SCHUBERT

---

[1] Ignaz Schuppanzigh (1776–1830) was the leader of a famous string quartet. When Beethoven first came to Vienna Schuppanzigh was his violin master.

65. TO THE PUBLISHER BERNHARD SCHOTT IN MAINZ

Vienna,
21*st February,* 1828

Dear Sir,

I am much honoured by your letter of February 8th, and am very pleased to enter into closer association with a firm of such repute, and one that is in a position to give publicity to my works abroad.

I have the following compositions on hand :

(*a*) Trio for pianoforte, violin and violoncello, which was performed with great success here.

(*b*) Two string quartets (in G major and D minor).

(*c*) Four impromptus for pianoforte alone, which could be published either separately or together.

(*d*) Fantasia for the pianoforte, arranged for four hands, dedicated to the Countess Caroline Esterhazy.

(*e*) Fantasia for pianoforte and violin.

(*f*) Songs for a single voice with pianoforte accompaniment. Poems by Schiller, Goethe, Klopstock, etc., etc., and Seidl, Schober, Leitner, Schulze, etc., etc.

(g) Quartets for both male and female voices with pianoforte accompaniment, of which two contain solo parts. Poems by Grillparzer and Seidl.

(h) A quintet for male voices. Poem by Schober.

(i) Battle song by Klopstock. Double chorus for eight male voices.

(j) Humorous trio : " The Wedding-breakfast " by Schober, for soprano, tenor and bass, which has already been performed with success.

This completes the list of my finished compositions : in addition I have written three Operas, a Mass and a Symphony. I only mention these last however in order to make known to you my efforts in the highest forms of musical art.

Should you care to consider for publication anything from the above list, I should be pleased to send it in return for a moderate remuneration.

With all respect,

FRANZ SCHUBERT

My address :
Unter den Tuchlauben,
at " The Blue Hedgehog ",
2nd floor.

66. TO THE SAME

Vienna,
10*th April,* 1828

Dear Sir,

The arrangements and prepara-
tions connected with my concert—which con-
sisted entirely of my own compositions—were
responsible for this long delay in replying to
your letter. In the meantime I have had
copies made of the trio for which you asked—
this was received by a crowded house with
such extraordinary enthusiasm that I have
been asked to repeat the concert—and also of
the impromptu and the quintet for male voices.
If you agree to the price of 100 Conventional
florins for this trio and 60 florins for the other
two works together, I can send them off at
once.   I would beg you, though, to have them
published as soon as possible.

With the greatest respect,

FRZ. SCHUBERT

67. TO PROBST

Vienna,
10*th April,* 1828

Dear Sir,

You have honoured me with a
letter which has been left unanswered up till

now by reason of the arrangements connected with my concert. It may perhaps interest you to hear that this concert, at which only my own compositions were performed, was given before a crowded audience, and that I myself received an extraordinarily enthusiastic reception. A trio for pianoforte, violin and violoncello roused such widespread interest that I have been invited to give a second concert (which will be a repetition more or less of the first). I shall, by the way, be very glad to let you have some of my compositions if you are prepared to pay the moderate sum of 60 Conventional florins for a good selection of the same. It is hardly necessary to assure you that I shall only submit what I consider to be really successful compositions—in so far as the composer himself and various select groups of friends are able to judge—for it is naturally a matter of the first importance to myself to send out nothing but really fine work into foreign countries.

With all respect,
Yours faithfully,
FRZ. SCHUBERT

N.B. My address is :
Unter den Tuchlauben,
at " The Blue Hedgehog ", 2nd floor.

68. TO THE SAME

Vienna,
10 *May,* 1828

Dear Sir,

I beg to send you herewith the trio for which you ask, although the suggested price of 60 conventional florins was intended for a book of songs or of pianoforte pieces— not for a trio which has six times as much work in it. However, in order at length to make a start, I beg you to hurry on with the publication as soon as may be, and to send me six copies. The closest attention should be paid to the abbreviated musical signs in the last piece. See that really capable players are found for the first performance, and above all see that, where the time changes in the last part, the rhythm is not lost. The minuet in moderate time, *piano* throughout ; but the trio on the contrary to be played with power except where it is marked *piano* or *pianissimo*. Awaiting the earliest publication of the same,

I remain,
with the greatest esteem,
yours faithfully,

FRZ. SCHUBERT

69. TO THE PUBLISHER BERNHARD SCHOTT IN
MAINZ

Vienna,
23rd May, 1828

Dear Sir,
        I beg to send you herewith the
two compositions for which you asked. The
price of each is 60 Conventional florins. I
do hope that they may be published as soon
as possible, and that you will do good business
with them : a permissible wish, since both
compositions have been very favourably
received here. Awaiting the receipt of the
promised honorarium,
                I remain
                        Yours respectfully,
                                FRZ. SCHUBERT
        N.B. I must ask you too for six copies of
each work.

70. TO PROBST.

[*Vienna,*
1*st August,* 1828]

Dear Sir,
        The trio is Opus 100. I beg you
to make sure that the edition is free from
errors. I am ardently looking forward to its

publication. This work will not be dedicated to any special person, but rather to all who find pleasure in it. That is the most profitable form of dedication.

With all respect,

FRZ. SCHUBERT

71. TO JOHANN BAPTIST JENGER

Vienna,

25th September, 1828

I have already given Haslinger the second part of the " Winter Journey ". This year I shall have to give up the journey to Grätz, for lack of money and bad weather are both wholly against it. I have much pleasure in accepting the invitation to visit Dr. Menz, for I am always very glad to hear Baron Schönstein sing. You will find me at Bogner's coffee-house in the Singerstrasse on Saturday afternoon between 4 and 5 o'clock.

Your friend,

SCHUBERT

My address is : Neue Wieden, Firmiansgasse No. 694, 2nd floor, right-hand side.

72. TO SCHOTT

Vienna,
2nd October, 1828

Dear Sir,

A considerable time has elapsed since your last letter, and I should be very glad to know if you have duly received the compositions which I sent by Haslinger, namely, four impromptus and a quintet for male voices. Will you kindly let me have an answer about this? I am especially anxious that these compositions should be published as soon as possible. The impromptus are Opus 101 : the quintet 102. Hoping for a quick and favourable reply,

With all respect,

FRZ. SCHUBERT

My address :
Neue Wieden, at the " Town of Ronsperg ",
No. 694 on the 2nd floor, right-hand side.

73. TO PROBST

Vienna,
2nd October, 1828

Dear Sir,

I am wondering if the trio will ever appear? Are you still without its number ? It is Opus 100. I am anxiously awaiting its publication. I have composed among other things three sonatas for pianoforte alone, which I want to dedicate to Hummel. I have also set to music several lyrics by Heine [1] which have had an extraordinarily good reception here, and finally I have written a quintet for 2 violins, 1 viola and 2 violoncelli. I have played the sonata in several places with great success, but the quintet rehearsal will only begin in the next few days. Should any of these compositions by any chance commend themselves to you, please let me know.

I sign myself,

With all respect,

FRZ. SCHUBERT

My address is : Neue Wieden, No. 694, at the " Town of Ronsperg ", 2nd floor, right-hand side.

---

[1] Heinrich Heine, the famous Rhineland poet, was at that time living in Hamburg.

74. TO SCHOBER

Vienna,
12*th November*, 1828

Dear Schober,

I am ill. I have had nothing to eat or drink for eleven days now, and can only wander feebly and uncertainly between armchair and bed. Rinna is treating me.[1] If I take any food I cannot retain it at all.

So please be so good as to come to my aid in this desperate condition with something to read. I have read Cooper's " Last of the Mohicans ", " The Spy ", " The Pilot ", and " The Pioneers ". If by any chance you have anything else of his, I beg you to leave it for me at the coffee-house with Frau von Bogner. My brother, who is conscientiousness itself, will bring it over to me without fail. Or indeed anything else.

Your friend,

SCHUBERT

[1] Schubert had been in bad health since September. On November 11th his illness took a more serious turn. The Court physician, Ernst Rinna von Sarenbach, who was attending him, fell ill himself, and other medical advisers were called in. On the 16th Schubert developed typhus, and at three o'clock in the afternoon of November 19th he died.